OXFORD

PICTURE

DICTIONARY

THIRD EDITION

Jayme Adelson-Goldstein
Norma Shapiro

OXFORD
UNIVERSITY PRESS

198 Madison Avenue
New York, NY 10016 USA

Great Clarendon Street, Oxford OX2 6DP, United Kingdom

Oxford University Press is a department of the University of Oxford.
It furthers the University's objective of excellence in research, scholarship,
and education by publishing worldwide. Oxford is a registered trade
mark of Oxford University Press in the UK and in certain other countries

© Oxford University Press 2016

The moral rights of the author have been asserted

First published in 2016
2020 2019 2018 2017
10 9 8 7 6 5 4

Photocopying

ISBN: 978 0 19 450529 1

Printed in China

This book is printed on paper from certified and well-managed sources

ACKNOWLEDGMENTS

Illustrations by: Lori Anzalone: 13, 70-71, 76-77; Joe "Fearless" Arenella/Will
Sumpter: 196; Argosy Publishing: 66-67 (call-outs), 108-109, 114-115
(call-outs), 156, 196, 205, 206-207, 215; Barbara Bastian: 4, 15, 208; Philip
Batini/AA Reps: 50; Thomas Bayley/Sparks Literary Agency: 162; Sally Bensusen:
217, 220; Peter Bollinger/Shannon Associates: 14-15; Higgens Bond/Anita Grien:
232; Molly Borman-Pullman: 118, 119; Mark Duffin: 7, 37, 61, 94, 238, 239, 240,
241; Jim Fanning/Ravenhill Represents: 80-81; Mike Gardner: 10, 12, 17, 22, 134,
116-117, 145-146, 179, 225, 234-235; Garth Glazier/AA Reps: 106, 111, 120; Dennis
Godfrey/Mike Wepplo: 214; Steve Graham: 126-127, 230; Julia Green/Mendola Art:
231; Glenn Gustafson: 9, 27, 48, 76, 100, 101, 119, 134-135, 138, 159, 165, 197;
Barbara Harmon: 218-219, 221; Ben Hasler/NB Illustration: 94-95, 101, 174, 188,
198-199; Betsy Hayes: 136, 140, 143; Matthew Holmes: 75; Stewart Holmes/
Illustration Ltd.: 204; Janos Jantner/Beehive Illustration: 5, 13, 82-83, 124-125,
132-133, 152-153, 166-167, 168, 169, 174, 175, 182-183, 192, 193; Ken Joudrey/
Munro Campagna: 52, 68-69, 187; Bob Kaganich/Deborah Wolfe: 10, 40-41, 123;
Steve Karp: 237, 238; Mike Kasun/Munro Campagna: 224; Graham Kennedy: 27;
Marcel Laverdet/AA Reps: 23; Jeffrey Lindberg: 33, 42-43, 92-93, 135, 164-165,
176-177, 186; Dennis Lyall/Artworks: 208; Chris Lyons/Lindgren & Smith: 203;
Alan Male/Artworks: 216, 217; Jeff Mangiat/Mendola Art: 53, 54, 55, 56, 57, 58, 59,
66-67; Adrian Mateescu/The Studio: 200-201, 238-239; Karen Minot: 28-29; Paul
Mirocha/The Wiley Group: 206, 222-223; Peter Miserendino/P.T. Pie Illustrations:
208; Lee Montgomery/Illustration Ltd.: 4; OUP Design: 20-21; Roger Motzkus: 235;
Laurie O'Keefe: 112, 222-223; Daniel O'Leary/Illustration Ltd.: 8-9, 26, 34-35, 78, 137,
138-139, 244; Vilma Ortiz-Dillon: 16, 20-21, 60, 98-99, 100, 217; Terry Pazcko: 46-47,
148-149, 156, 194, 233; David Preiss/Munro Campagna: 5; Pronk & Associates: 204-
205; Tony Randazzo/AA Reps: 160, 240-241; Mike Renwick/Creative Eye: 128-129;
Mark Riedy/Scott Hull Associates: 48-49, 79, 142, 157; Jon Rogers/AA Reps: 114; Jeff
Sanson/Schumann & Co.: 84-85, 246-247; Ben Shannon/Magnet Reps: 11, 64-65, 90,
91, 96, 97, 121, 147, 170-171, 172-173, 180-181, 245; Reed Sprunger/Jae Wagoner
Artists Rep.: 18-19, 238-239; Studio Liddell/AA Reps: 27; Angelo Tillary: 108-109;
Samuel Velasco/5W Infographics: 10, 11, 12, 13, 15, 48, 49, 80-81 (design), 110, 112,
113, 138, 143, 146, 156, 159, 210, 211, 212-213; Ralph Voltz/Deborah Wolfe: 50-51,
130-131, 144, 158, 163, 185, 190, 191, 207 (top left), 215 (bot. left), 242-243; Jeff Wack/
Mendola Art: 24, 25, 86-87, 102-103, 136-137, 237; Brad Walker: 104-105, 154-155,
161, 226-227; Wendy Wassink: 112-113; John White/The Neis Group: 209;

Eric Wilkerson: 32, 140; Simon Williams/Illustration Ltd.: 2-3, 6-7, 30-31, 36, 38-39,
44-45, 72-73, 141, 178, 184; Lee Woodgate/Eye Candy Illustration: 228-229; Andy Zito:
62-23; Craig Zuckerman: 14, 88-89, 114-115, 122-123, 206-207.

Cover Design: Studio Montage
Chapter icons designed by Anna Sereda

Commissioned studio photography for Oxford University Press done by Dennis
Kitchen Studio: 37, 61, 72, 73, 74, 75, 95, 96, 100, 189, 194, 195, 232.

*The publishers would like to thank the following for their kind permission to reproduce
photographs:* 20-21 (calender) dikobraziy/Shutterstock; 26 (penny) rsooll/
Shutterstock, (nickel) B.A.E. Inc./Alamy Stock Photo, (dime) Brandon Laufenberg/
istockphoto, (quarter) magicoven/Shutterstock, (half dollar) mattesimages/
Shutterstock, (Sacagawea dollar) Ted Foxx/Alamy Stock Photo; 31 (flowers photo)
Digital Vision/OUP; 48 (apartment interior) Sindre Ellingsen/Alamy Stock Photo;
61 (oven) gerenme/Getty Images; (table) Stefano Mattia/Getty Images, (window)
nexus 7/Shutterstock, (shower) FOTOGRAFIA INC./Getty Images, (dishes) Nika Art/
Shutterstock, (kitchen counter/sink) zstock/Shutterstock; 94 (watch) WM_idea/
Shutterstock; 98 (cotton texture) Saksan Maneechay/123RF, (linen texture)
daizuoxin/Shutterstock, (wool texture) riekephotos/Shutterstock, (cashmere texture)
ovb64/Shutterstock, (silk texture) Anteromite/Shutterstock, (leather texture) Victor
Newman/Shutterstock; 99 (denim) Jaroslaw Grudzinski/123RF, (suede) KPG Payless2/
Shutterstock, (lace) Nataliia Melnychuk/Shutterstock, (velvet) Neirfy/Shutterstock,
(corduroy) Eldad Carin/Shutterstock, (nylon) B Calkins/Shutterstock; 141 (Pentagon)
Don S. Montgomery/Corbis; 208 (civil rights) PhotoQuest/Contributor/Getty
Images, (Civil War) Philip Gould/Corbis, (Great Depression) Rolls Press/Popperfoto/
Contributor/Getty Images, (Industrial Revolution) Mary Evans Picture Library/
Alamy Stock Photo, (Jazz Age) Underwood & Underwood/Underwood & Underwood/
Corbis, (Progressivism) AS400 DB/Corbis, (Reconstruction) MPI/Stringer/Getty
Images, (Spage Age) AFP/Stringer/Getty Images, (Western Expansion) AS400 DB/
Corbis, (WWI) ASSOCIATED PRESS, (WWII) Joe Rosenthal/Associated Press; 212
(thoughtful woman) Di Studio/Shutterstock; 213 (people in uniform) Rawpixel.com/
Shutterstock; 232 (tent) Hurst Photo/Shutterstock, (campfire) wolv/Getty Images;
244 (flute) cowardlion/Shutterstock, (clarinet) Vereshchagin Dmitry/Shutterstock,
(oboe) Matthias G. Ziegler/Shutterstock, (bassoon) Rodrigo Blanco/Getty Images,
(saxophone) Ocean/OUP, (violin) Ocean/OUP, (cello) Stockbyte/Getty Images, (bass) the
palms/Shutterstock, (guitar) Photodisc/OUP, (trombone) seen/Shutterstock, (trumpet)
Photodisc/OUP, (tuba) Ingram/OUP, (French horn) Venus Angel/Shutterstock, (piano)
liangpv/Getty Images, (xylophone) Yuri Kevhiev/Alamy Stock Photo, (drums) lem/
Shutterstock, (tambourine) Vereshchagin Dmitry/Shutterstock, (keyboard) George
Peters/Getty Images, (accordion) Stockbyte/Getty Images, (organ) C Squared Studios/
Getty Images, (harmonica) Goran Bogicevic/Alamy Stock Photo.

*The publisher would like to thank the following for their permission to reproduce
copyrighted material:*
127, 136–137: USPS Corporate Signature, Priority Mail, Express Mail, Media Mail,
Certified Mail, Ready Post, Airmail, Parcel Post, Letter Carrier Uniform, Postal Clerk
Uniform, Flag and Statue of Liberty, Postmark, Post Office Box, Automated Postal
Center, Parcel Drop Box, Round Top Collection Mailbox are trademarks of the United
States Postal Service and are used with permission. Flag and Statue of Liberty © 2006
United States Postal Service. All Rights Reserved. Used with Permission. 156:
MetroCard and the logo "MTA" are registered trademarks of the Metropolitan
Transportation Authority. Used with permission. 156: Metro token image courtesy of
LA Metro ©2016 LACMTA. 156: Amtrak ticket image courtesy of Amtrak. 174: National
Center for O*NET Development. O*NET OnLine. Retrieved November 23, 2015, from
https://www.onetonline.org/. 191: Microsoft Word® is a registered trademark of
Microsoft Corporation. Screen shot reprinted with permission from Microsoft
Corporation. 191: Microsoft Excel® is a registered trademark of Microsoft Corporation.
Screen shot reprinted with permission from Microsoft Corporation. 191: Microsoft
PowerPoint® is a registered trademark of Microsoft Corporation. Screen shot reprinted
with permission from Microsoft Corporation. 210: Microsoft icons reprinted by
permission of Microsoft.

This third edition of the Oxford Picture
Dictionary is lovingly dedicated to the
memory of Norma Shapiro.

Her ideas, her pictures, and her stories
continue to teach, inspire, and delight.

Acknowledgments

The publisher and authors would like to acknowledge the following individuals for their invaluable feedback during the development of this program:

Nawal Abbas, Lawrence Tech University, MI; Dr. Macarena Aguilar, Cy-Fair College, TX; Penny Aldrich, Durham Technical Community College, NC; Deanna Allen, Round Rock ISD, TX; Angela Andrade-Holt, Western Nevada College, NV; Joseph F. Anselme, Atlantic Technical Center, FL; Stacy Antonopoulos, Monterey Trail High School, CA; Carol Antunano, The English Center, FL; Irma Arencibia, Thomas A. Edison School, NJ; Stephanie Austin, CBET Program Moreland School District, CA; Suzi Austin, Alexandria City Public School Adult Program, FL; Carol Beebe, Niagara University, NY; Patricia S. Bell, Lake Technical Center, FL; Derick Bonewitz, College of Lake County, IL; Emily Box, Granite Peaks Learning Center, UT; Diana Brady-Herndon, Western Nevada College, NV; Jim Brice, San Diego Community College District, CA; Theresa Bries, Black Hawk College, IL; Diane Brody, St. John's Lutheran Church; Mindy Bruton, Abilene ISD, TX; Caralyn Bushey, Montgomery College TESOL Certificate Program, MD; Phil Cackley, Arlington Education and Employment Program (REEP), VA; Frieda Caldwell, Metropolitan Adult Education Program, CA; Anne Marie Caney, Chula Vista Adult School, CA; Lynda Cannon, Ashland Community and Technical College, KY; Lenore Cardoza, Brockton Public Schools Adult Learning Center, MA; Victor Castellanos, Covina Public Library, CA; Marjorie Castillo-Farquhar, Community Action/Austin Community College, TX; Patricia Castro, Harvest English Institute, NJ; Paohui Lola Chen, Milpitas Adult School, CA; Alicia Chicas, The Hayward Center for Education & Careers (Adult School), CA; Michelle Chuang, East Side Adult Education, CA; Lori Cisneros, Atlantic Vo-Tech, FL; Joyce Clapp, Hayward Adult School, CA; Stacy Clark, Arlington Education and Employment Program (REEP), VA; Melissa Cohen, Literacy New Jersey - Middlesex Programs, NJ; Dave Coleman, LAUSD District, CA; Edith Cowper, Wake Technical Community College, NC; Leslie Crawley, The Literacy Center; Kelli Crow, City College San Francisco Civic Center, CA; Nancy B. Crowell, Southside Programs for Adults in Continuing Education, VA; Doroti da Cunha, Hialeah-Miami Lakes Adult Education Center, FL; Brenda Custodio, Ohio State University, OH; Dory Dannettell, Community Educational Outreach, CO; Paula Da Silva-Michelin, La Guardia Community College, NY; Peggy Datz, Berkeley Adult School, CA; Cynthia L. Davies, Humble I.S.D., TX; Christopher Davis, Overfelt Adult Center, CA; Laura De Anda, Margaret Aylward Center, CA; Tyler Degener, Drexel University College of Medicine, PA; Jacquelyn Delaney; Mariana De Luca, Charlotte-Mecklenburg Public Schools, NC; Georgia Deming, Johnson County Community College (JCAE), KS; Beverly De Nicola, Capistrano Unified School District, CA; Irena Dewey, US Conversation; Frances Tornabene De Sousa, Pittsburg Adult Education Center, CA; Matthew Diamond, The University of Texas at Austin, TX; Beatriz Diaz, Miami-Dade County Public Schools, FL; Druci Diaz, Program Advisor, Adult & Career Services Center Hillsborough County Public Schools, FL; Natalya Dollar, North Orange County Community College District, CA; Marion Donahue, San Dieguito Adult School, CA; Nick Doorn, International Education Services, MI; Mercedes Douglass, Seminole Community College, FL; Joan Dundas, Brock University, ON (Canada); Jennifer Eick-Magán, Prairie State College, IL; Jenny Elliott, Montgomery College, MD; Paige Endo, Mt. Diablo Adult Education, CA; Megan Ernst, Glendale Community College, CA; Elizabeth Escobar, Robert Waters School, NJ; Joanne Everett, Dave Thomas Education Center, FL; Jennifer Fadden, Arlington Education and Employment Program (REEP), VA; Cinzia Fagan, East Side Adult Education, CA; Jacqui Farrell, Literacy Volunteers on the Green, CT; Ross Feldberg, Tufts University, MA; Sharyl Ferguson, Montwood High School, TX; Emily Finch, FCI Englewood, CO; Dr. Robert Finkelstein, Willammette Dental, OR; Janet Fischer, Lawrence Public Schools - Adult Learning Center, MA; Dr. Monica Fishkin, University of Central Florida, FL; Jan Foley, Wilbur Wright College - City Colleges of Chicago, IL; Tim Foster, Silver Valley Adult Education Center, CA; Nancy Frampton, Reedley College, CA; Lynn A. Freeland, San Dieguito Union High School District, CA; Sally A. Fox, East Side Adult Education, CA; Cathy Gample, San Leandro Adult School, CA; Hillary Gardner, Center for Immigrant Education and Training, NY; Elizabeth Gibb, Castro Valley Adult and Career Education, CA; Martha C. Giffen, Alhambra Unified School District, CA; Elgy Gillespie, City College San Francisco, CA; Lisa Marcelle Gimbel, Community Learning Center, MA; Jill Gluck, Hollywood Community Adult School, CA; Richard Goldberg, Asian American Civic Association, MA; Carolyn Grebe, The Hayward Center for Education & Careers (Adult School), CA; Carolyn Grimaldi, LaGuardia Community College, NY; Cassell Gross, Intercambio, CO; William Gruenholz, USD Adult School, CA; Sandra G. Gutierrez, Hialeah-Miami Lakes Adult Education Center, FL; Conte Gúzman-Hoffman, Triton College, IL; William J. Hall, M.D. FACP/FRSM (UK); Amanda Harllee, Palmetto High School, FL; Kathy Harris, Portland State University, OR; Kay Hartley, Fairfield-Suisun Adult School, CA; Melissa Hassmann, Northwest Iowa Community College, IA; Mercedes Hearn, Tampa Bay Technical Center, FL; Christyann Helm, Carlos Rosario International Public Charter School, WA; Suzanne Hibbs, East Side Adult Education, CA; Lindsey Himanga, Hiawatha Valley ABE, MN; Marvina Hooper, Lake Technical College, FL; Jill A. Horohoe, Arizona State University, AZ; Roxana Hurtado, Miami Dade Adult, FL; Rachel Johnson, MORE Multicultural School for Empowerment, MN; Randy Johnson, Hartford Public Library, CT; Sherry Joseph, Miami Dade College, FL; Elaine Kanakis, The Hayward Center for Education and Careers, CA; Phoebe Kang, Brock University, ON (Canada); Mary Kaufman, Brewster Technical Center, FL; Jeanne Kearsley, City College San Francisco Chinatown, CA; Sallyann Kovacs, The Hayward Center for Education & Careers (Adult School), CA; Jennifer Latzgo, Lehigh Carbon Community College, PA; Sandy Lawler, East Side Adult Education, CA; Xinhua Li, City College of San Francisco, CA; Renata Lima, TALK International School of Languages, FL; Luz M. Lopez, Sweetwater Union High School District, CA; Osmara Lopez, Bronx Community College, NY; Heather Lozano, North Lake College, TX; Marcia Luptak, Elgin Community College, IL; Betty Lynch, Arlington Education and Employment Program (REEP), VA; Matthew Lyter, Tri-County OIC, PA; Meera Madan, REID Park Elementary School, NC; Julia Maffei, Texas State IEP, TX; Ivanna Mann Thrower, Charlotte Mecklenburg Schools, NC; Anna Mariani, The English Center (TLC Online), FL; Michael R. Mason, Loma Technical Adult Center, CA; Terry Masters, American Schools of Water for Ishmael, OH; Debbie Matsumura, CBET Program Moreland School District, CA; Holley Mayville, Charlotte Mecklenburg Schools, NC; Margaret McCabe, United Methodist Cooperative Ministries, FL; David McCarthy, Stony Brook University, NY; Todd McDonald, Hillsborough Adult Education, FL; Nancy A. McKeand, ESL Consultant, LA; Rebecca L. McLain, Gaston College, NC; John M. Mendoza, Redlands Adult School, CA; Nancy Meredith, Austin Community College, TX; Marcia Merriman, Community College of Baltimore County, MD; Bet Messmer, Santa Clara Adult Education Center, CA; Holly Milkowart, Johnson County Community College, KS; Jose Montes, The English Center M-DCPS, FL; Elaine Moore, Escondido Adult School, CA; Lisa Munoz, Metropolitan Education District, CA; Mary Murphy-Clagett, Sweetwater Union High School District, CA; Jonetta Myles, Rockdale County High School, GA; Marwan Nabi, Troy High School, CA; Dale Nave, San Marcos Academy, TX; Dr. Christine L. Nelsen, Salvation Army Community Center, FL; Michael W. Newman, Arlington Education and Employment Program (REEP), VA; Virginia Nicolai, Colorado Mountain College, CO; Phoebe Nip, East Side Adult Education, CA; Rehana Nusrat, Huntington Beach Adult School, CA; Cindy Oakley-Paulik, Embry-Riddle Aeronautical University, FL; Judy O'Louglin, CATESOL, CA; Brigitte Oltmanns, Triton College, IL; Nora Onayemi, Montgomery College, MD; Lorena Orozco, Catholic Charities, NM; Allison Pickering, Escondido Adult School, CA; Odette Petrini, Huron High School, MI; Eileen Purcell, Clatsop Community College, OR; Teresa Reen, East Side Adult Education, CA; Jean Renoll, Fairfax County Public Schools – ACE, VA; Carmen Rivera-Diaz, Calvary Church; Fatiana Roganova, The Hayward Center for Education & Careers (Adult School), CA; Rosa Rojo, Escondido Adult School, CA; Lorraine Romero, Houston Community College, TX; Phoebe B. Rouse, Louisiana State University, LA; Dr. Susan Rouse, Southern Wesleyan University, SC; Blair Roy, Chapman Education Center, CA; Sharon Saylors, The Hayward Center for Education & Careers (Adult School), CA; Margret Schaefer, Round Rock ISD, TX; Arlene R. Schwartz, Broward Community Schools, FL; Geraldyne Blake Scott, Truman College, IL; Sharada Sekar, Antioch High School Freshman Academy, TN; Denise Selleck, City College San Francisco Civic Center, CA; Dr. Cheryl J. Serrano, Lynn University, FL; Janet Setzekorn, United Methodist Cooperative Ministries, FL; Terry Shearer, EDUCALL Learning Services, TX; Rob Sheppard, Quincy Asian Resources, Inc., MA; Dr. Ira M. Sheskin, University of Miami, FL; Glenda Sinks, Community College of Denver, CO; Elisabeth Sklar, Township High School District 113, IL; Jacqueline Sport, LBWCC Luverne Center, AL; Kathryn Spyksma, The Hayward Center for Education & Careers (Adult School), CA; Linda Steele, Black Hawk College, IL; Robert Stein, BEGIN Managed Programs, NY; Martin Steinman, Canal Alliance, CA; Ruth Sutton, Township High School District 113, IL; Alisa Takeuchi, Chapman Education Center, CA; Grace Tanaka, Santa Ana College School of Continuing Education, CA; Annalisa Te, East Side Adult Education, CA; Oscar Tellez, Daley College, IL; Fotini Terzi, University of Texas at Austin, TX; Geneva Tesh, Houston Community College, TX; Maiko Tomizawa, D.D.S., NY; Don Torluemke, South Bay Adult School, CA; Francisco Torres, Olive-Harvey College, IL; Shawn Tran, East Side Adult Education, CA; Serife Turkol, Literary Council of Northern Virginia, VA; Cristina Urena, CC/Tech Center, FL; Maliheh Vafai, East Side Adult Education, CA; Charlotte van Londen, MCAEL, MD; Tara Vasquez, Robert Waters School, NJ; Nina Velasco, Naples Language Center, FL; Colin Ward, Lone Star College-North Harris, TX; Theresa Warren, East Side Adult Center, CA; Lucie Gates Watel, Truman College, IL; Wendy Weil, Arnold Middle School, TX; Patricia Weist, TALK International School of Languages, FL; Dr. Carole Lynn Weisz, Lehman College, NY; Desiree Wesner, Robert Waters School, NJ; David Wexler, Napa Valley Adult School, CA; Kathy Wiersema, Black Hawk College, IL; Cynthia Wiseman, Borough of Manhattan Community College, NY; Nancy Whitmire, University of Arkansas Community College at Batesville, AR; Debbie Cullinane Wood, Lincoln Education Center, CA; Banu Yaylali, Miami Dade College, FL; Hongyan Zheng, Milpitas Adult Education, Milpitas, CA; Yelena Zimon, Fremont Adult and Continuing Education, CA; Arlene Zivitz, ESOL Teacher, FL

Table of Contents

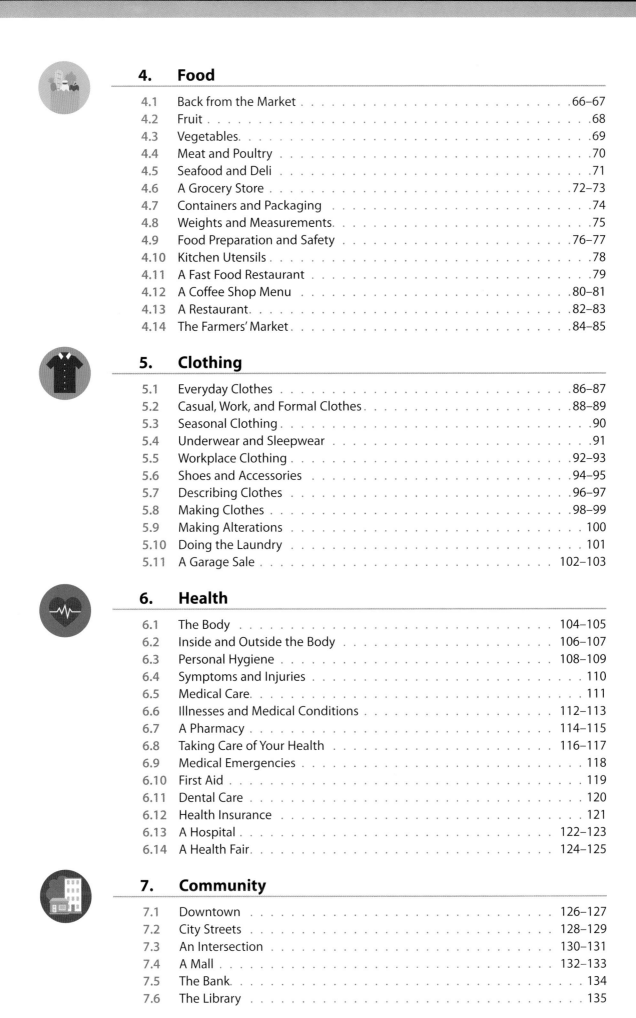

Contents

11. Academic Study

12. Recreation

The Oxford Picture Dictionary **Third Edition provides unparalleled support for vocabulary teaching and language development.**

- Illustrations present over 4,000 English words and phrases within **meaningful, real-life contexts**.
- **New and expanded topics** including job search, career planning, and digital literacy prepare students to meet the requirements of their daily lives.
- Updated activities prepare students for **work, academic study, and citizenship**.
- **Oxford 3000 vocabulary** ensures students learn the most useful and important words.

Color coding and icons make it easy to navigate through *OPD*.

Vibrant illustrations and rich contexts improve vocabulary acquisition.

Subtopics present the words in easy-to-learn "chunks."

Revised practice activities help students develop academic and workforce skills.

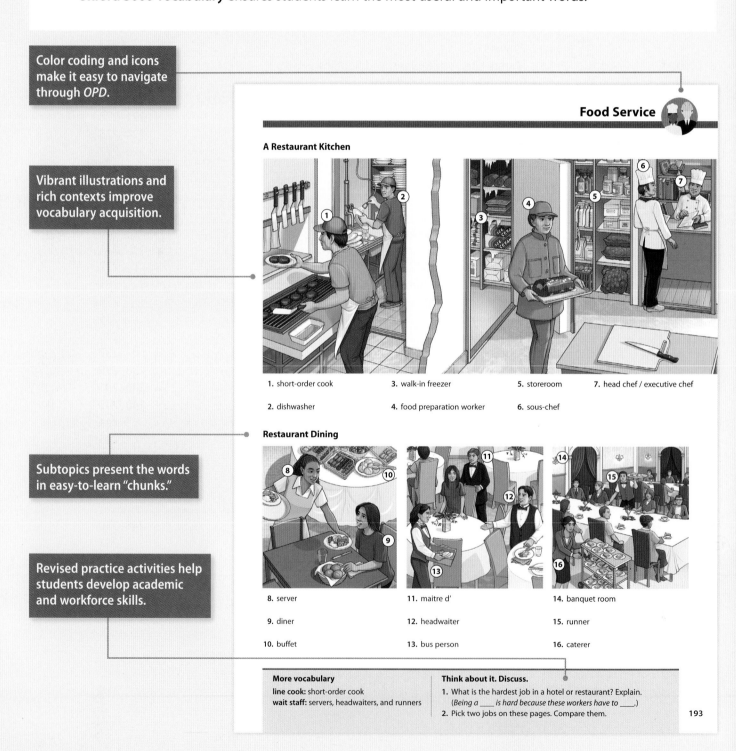

Food Service

A Restaurant Kitchen

1. short-order cook
2. dishwasher
3. walk-in freezer
4. food preparation worker
5. storeroom
6. sous-chef
7. head chef / executive chef

Restaurant Dining

8. server
9. diner
10. buffet
11. maitre d'
12. headwaiter
13. bus person
14. banquet room
15. runner
16. caterer

More vocabulary
line cook: short-order cook
wait staff: servers, headwaiters, and runners

Think about it. Discuss.
1. What is the hardest job in a hotel or restaurant? Explain.
   (*Being a ____ is hard because these workers have to ____.*)
2. Pick two jobs on these pages. Compare them.

193

Intro pages open each unit with key vocabulary related to the unit theme. Clear, engaging artwork promotes questions, conversations, and writing practice for all levels.

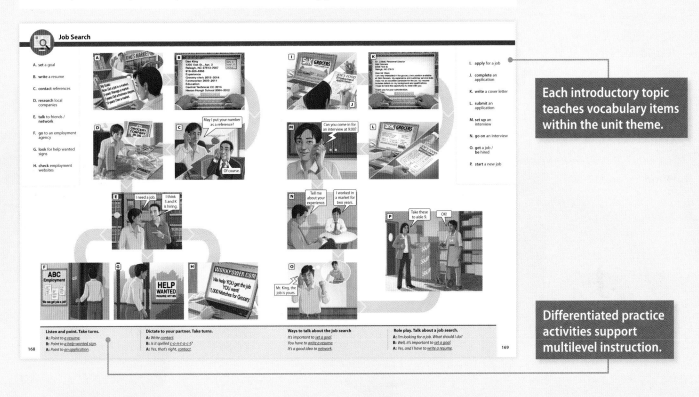

Each introductory topic teaches vocabulary items within the unit theme.

Differentiated practice activities support multilevel instruction.

Story pages close each unit with a lively scene for reviewing vocabulary and teaching additional language. Meanwhile, rich visual contexts recycle words from the unit.

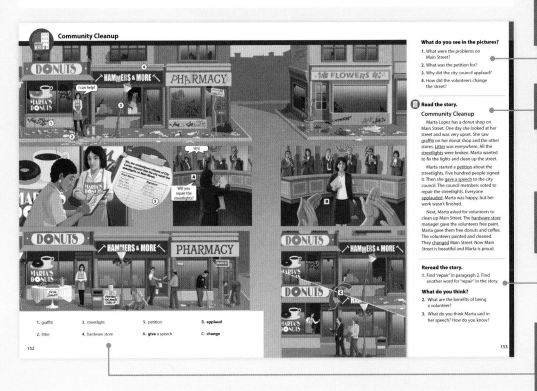

Pre-reading questions build students' previewing and predicting skills.

End-of-unit readings promote literacy skills.

Post-reading questions support critical thinking and textual analysis skills.

The word list previews key vocabulary that students will encounter in the story.

Meeting and Greeting

A. **Say**, "Hello."

B. **Ask**, "How are you?"

C. **Respond**, "Fine, thanks."

D. **Introduce** yourself.

E. **Smile**.

F. **Hug**.

G. **Wave**.

Tell your partner what to do. Take turns.

1. *Say, "Hello."*
2. *Bow.*
3. *Smile.*
4. *Shake hands.*
5. *Wave.*
6. *Say, "Goodbye."*

Dictate to your partner. Take turns.

A: *Write smile.*
B: *Is it spelled s-m-i-l-e?*
A: *Yes, that's right.*

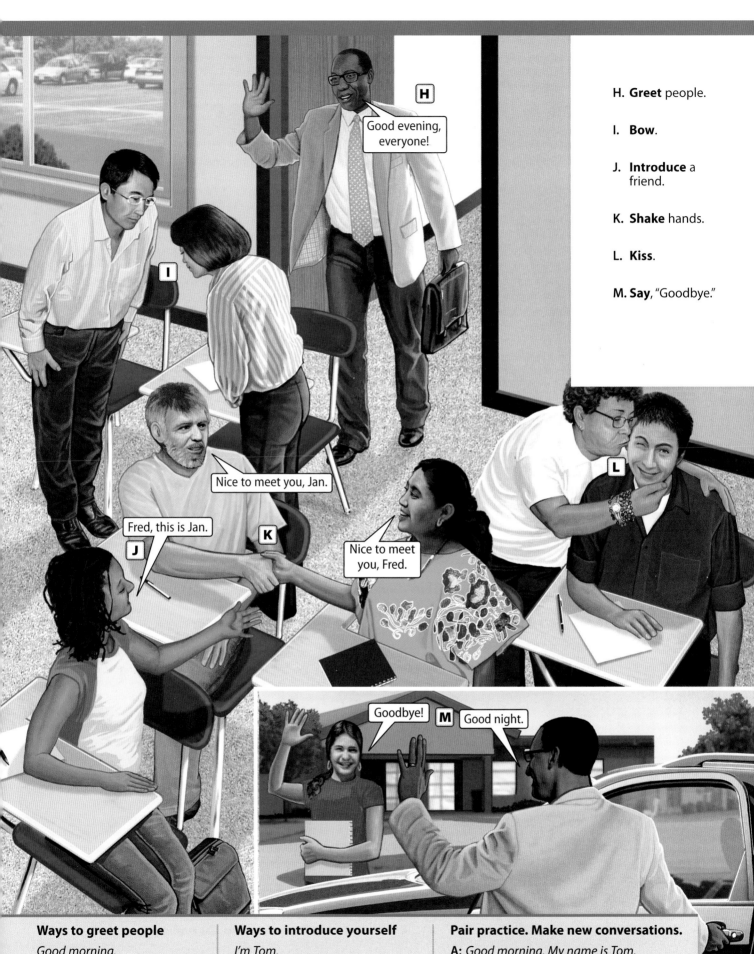

H. **Greet** people.

I. **Bow**.

J. **Introduce** a friend.

K. **Shake** hands.

L. **Kiss**.

M. **Say**, "Goodbye."

Ways to greet people	**Ways to introduce yourself**	**Pair practice. Make new conversations.**
Good morning.	*I'm <u>Tom</u>.*	**A:** *Good morning. My name is <u>Tom</u>.*
Good afternoon.	*My name is <u>Tom</u>.*	**B:** *Nice to meet you, <u>Tom</u>. I'm <u>Sara</u>.*
Good evening.	*Hello. I'm <u>Tom Muñoz</u>.*	**A:** *Nice to meet you, <u>Sara</u>.*

Personal Information

A. **Say** your name.

B. **Spell** your name.

C. **Print** your name.

D. **Type** your name.

E. **Sign** your name.

Filling Out a Form

(813) 555-1234 ⑩ ⑪

(813) 555-5005 ⑫

(813) 555-8976 ⑬

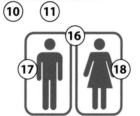

⑳ Carlos R. Soto

---

https://www.registrationformOPD.com

1. name

2. first name   3. middle initial   4. last name

address

5. street address   6. apartment number   7. city   8. state   9. ZIP code

work phone

( ) -   **additional numbers**   ( ) -   ( ) -

10. area code   11. phone number   12. home phone   13. cell phone

14. date of birth (DOB)   15. place of birth (POB)   16. gender   17. male   18. female   19. Social Security number

20. signature

Pair practice. Make new conversations.

A: *My first name is Carlos.*
B: *Please spell Carlos for me.*
A: *C-a-r-l-o-s.*

Internet Research: popular names

Type "SSA, top names 100 years" in the search bar.
Report: *According to the SSA list, James is the number 1 male name.*

Campus

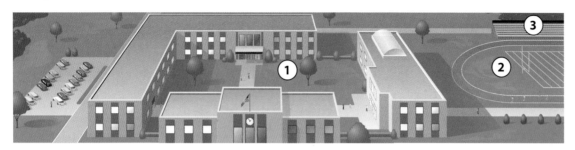

1. quad
2. field
3. bleachers
4. principal
5. assistant principal
6. counselor
7. classroom
8. teacher
9. restrooms
10. hallway
11. locker
12. main office
13. clerk
14. cafeteria
15. computer lab
16. teacher's aide
17. library
18. auditorium
19. gym
20. coach
21. track

Administrators

Around Campus

More vocabulary

Students do not pay to attend a **public school**.

Students pay to attend a **private school**.

A church, mosque, or temple school is a **parochial school**.

Use contractions and talk about the pictures.

He **is** = He**'s**   She **is** = She**'s**

It **is** = It**'s**   They **are** = They**'re**

He's a teacher.   *They're* students.

1. whiteboard
2. screen
3. chalkboard
4. teacher / instructor
5. LCD projector
6. student
7. desk
8. headphones

A. **Raise** your hand.

B. **Talk** to the teacher.

C. **Listen** to a recording.

D. **Stand up**.

E. **Write** on the board.

F. **Sit down**. / **Take** a seat.

G. **Open** your book.

H. **Close** your book.

I. **Pick up** the pencil.

J. **Put down** the pencil.

ABCDEFGHIJKLMNOPQRSTUVWXYZ

9. clock

10. bookcase

11. chair

12. map

13. alphabet

14. bulletin board

15. computer

16. document camera

17. dry erase marker

18. chalk

19. eraser

20. pencil

21. (pencil) eraser

22. pen

23. pencil sharpener

24. permanent marker

25. highlighter

26. textbook

27. workbook

28. 3-ring binder / notebook

29. notebook paper

30. spiral notebook

31. learner's dictionary

32. picture dictionary

Grammar Point: *there is / there are*

*There **is a** map.*   *There **are 15** students.*

Describe your classroom. Take turns.

A: *There's <u>a clock</u>.*   B: *There are <u>20 chairs</u>.*

Survey your class. Record the responses.

1. Do you prefer pens or pencils?
2. Do you prefer talking or listening?

Report: *Most of us... Some of us...*

Learning New Words

A. **Look up** the word.

B. **Read** the definition.

C. **Translate** the word.

D. **Check** the pronunciation.

E. **Copy** the word.

F. **Draw** a picture.

Working with Your Classmates

G. **Discuss** a problem.

H. **Brainstorm** solutions / answers.

I. **Work** in a group.

J. **Help** a classmate.

Working with a Partner

K. **Ask** a question.　　L. **Answer** a question.

M. **Share** a book.

N. **Dictate** a sentence.

Following Directions

O. **Fill in** the blank.

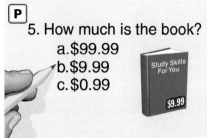

P. **Choose** the correct answer.

Q. **Circle** the answer.

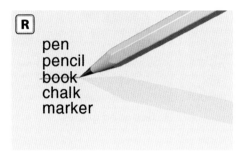

R. **Cross out** the word.

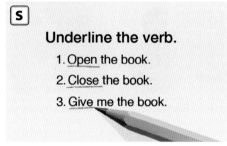

S. **Underline** the word.

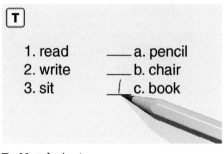

T. **Match** the items.

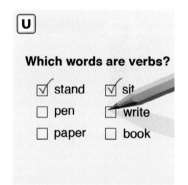

U. **Check** the correct boxes.

V. **Label** the picture.

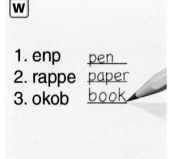

W. **Unscramble** the words.

X. **Put** the sentences in order.

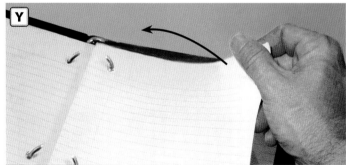

Y. **Take out** a piece of paper.

Z. **Put away** your books.

Survey your class. Record the responses.

1. Do you prefer to study in a group or with a partner?
2. Do you prefer to translate or draw new words?

Report: *Most of us… Some of us…*

Identify Tom's problem. Brainstorm solutions.

Tom wants to study English with a group. He wants to ask his classmates, "Do you want to study together?" but he's embarrassed.

Ways to Succeed

A. Set goals.

B. Participate in class.

C. Take notes.

D. Study at home.

E. Pass a test.

F. Ask for help. / **Request** help.

G. Make progress.

H. Get good grades.

Taking a Test

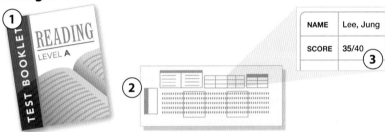

1. test booklet   2. answer sheet   3. score

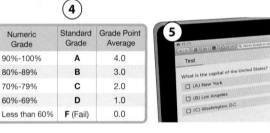

Numeric Grade	Standard Grade	Grade Point Average
90%-100%	A	4.0
80%-89%	B	3.0
70%-79%	C	2.0
60%-69%	D	1.0
Less than 60%	F (Fail)	0.0

4. grades   5. online test

I. Clear off your desk.

J. Work on your own.

K. Bubble in the answer.

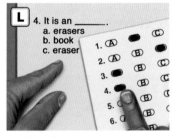

L. Check your work.

M. Erase the mistake.

N. Correct the mistake.

O. Hand in your test.

P. Submit your test.

A. **Walk** to class.

B. **Run** to class.

C. **Enter** the room.

D. **Turn on** the lights.

E. **Lift / Pick up** the books.

F. **Carry** the books.

G. **Deliver** the books.

H. **Take** a break.

I. **Eat**.

J. **Drink**.

K. **Buy** a snack.

L. **Have** a conversation.

M. **Go back** to class.

N. **Throw away** trash.

O. **Leave** the room.

P. **Turn off** the lights.

Grammar Point: present continuous

Use **be** + <u>verb</u> + **ing** (What **are** they <u>**doing**</u>?)
He **is walking**. They **are talking**.
Note: run—run**ning**   leave—leav**ing** [e]

Look at the pictures. Describe what is happening.

A: They are <u>entering the room</u>.
B: He is <u>walking</u>.
C: She's <u>eating</u>.

11

Everyday Conversation

A. **start** a conversation

B. **make** small talk

C. **compliment** someone

D. **thank** someone

E. **offer** something

F. **refuse** an offer

G. **apologize**

H. **accept** an apology

I. **invite** someone

J. **accept** an invitation

K. **decline** an invitation

L. **agree**

M. **disagree**

N. **explain** something

O. **check** your understanding

More vocabulary

accept a compliment: to thank someone for a compliment

make a request: to ask for something

Pair practice. Follow the directions.

1. Start a conversation with your partner.
2. Make small talk with your partner.
3. Compliment each other.

Temperature

1. Fahrenheit
2. Celsius
3. hot
4. warm
5. cool
6. cold
7. freezing
8. degrees

A Weather Map

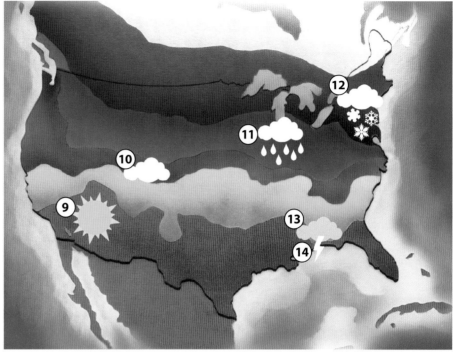

9. sunny / clear
10. cloudy
11. rain
12. snow
13. thunderstorm
14. lightning

Weather Conditions

15. heat wave

16. smoggy

17. humid

18. hurricane

19. windy

20. dust storm

21. foggy

22. hail

23. icy

24. snowstorm / blizzard

Ways to talk about the weather

It's <u>sunny</u> and <u>hot</u> in <u>Dallas</u>.
It's <u>raining</u> in <u>Chicago</u>.
<u>Rome</u> is having <u>thunderstorms</u>.

Internet Research: weather

Type any city and "weather" in the search bar.
Report: It's <u>cloudy</u> in <u>L.A.</u> It's <u>70 degrees</u>.

1. phone line

2. phone jack

3. base

4. handset / receiver

5. keypad

6. star key

7. pound key

8. cell phone

9. charger cord

10. charger plug

11. strong signal

12. weak signal

13. headset

14. Bluetooth headset

15. contact list

16. missed call

17. voice mail

18. text message

19. Internet phone call

20. operator

21. directory assistance

22. automated phone system

23. phone card

24. access number

25. smartphone

26. TDD*

Reading a Phone Bill

27. carrier

28. area code

29. phone number

30. billing period

31. monthly charges

32. additional charges

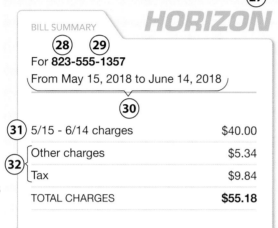

HORIZON

BILL SUMMARY

For **823-555-1357**
From May 15, 2018 to June 14, 2018

5/15 - 6/14 charges	$40.00
Other charges	$5.34
Tax	$9.84
TOTAL CHARGES	**$55.18**

Types of Charges

33. local call

34. long-distance call

35. international call

36. data

Making a Phone Call

A. **Dial** the phone number.

B. **Press** "talk".

C. **Talk** on the phone.

D. **Hang up**. / **End** the call.

Making an Emergency Call

E. **Dial** 911.

F. **Give** your name.

G. **State** the emergency.

H. **Stay** on the line.

*telecommunication device for the deaf

Numbers

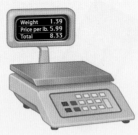

Cardinal Numbers

0	zero	20	twenty
1	one	21	twenty-one
2	two	22	twenty-two
3	three	23	twenty-three
4	four	24	twenty-four
5	five	25	twenty-five
6	six	30	thirty
7	seven	40	forty
8	eight	50	fifty
9	nine	60	sixty
10	ten	70	seventy
11	eleven	80	eighty
12	twelve	90	ninety
13	thirteen	100	one hundred
14	fourteen	101	one hundred one
15	fifteen	1,000	one thousand
16	sixteen	10,000	ten thousand
17	seventeen	100,000	one hundred thousand
18	eighteen	1,000,000	one million
19	nineteen	1,000,000,000	one billion

Ordinal Numbers

1st	first	16th	sixteenth
2nd	second	17th	seventeenth
3rd	third	18th	eighteenth
4th	fourth	19th	nineteenth
5th	fifth	20th	twentieth
6th	sixth	21st	twenty-first
7th	seventh	30th	thirtieth
8th	eighth	40th	fortieth
9th	ninth	50th	fiftieth
10th	tenth	60th	sixtieth
11th	eleventh	70th	seventieth
12th	twelfth	80th	eightieth
13th	thirteenth	90th	ninetieth
14th	fourteenth	100th	one hundredth
15th	fifteenth	1,000th	one thousandth

Roman Numerals

I = 1	VII = 7	XXX = 30
II = 2	VIII = 8	XL = 40
III = 3	IX = 9	L = 50
IV = 4	X = 10	C = 100
V = 5	XV = 15	D = 500
VI = 6	XX = 20	M = 1,000

A. **divide**

B. **calculate**

C. **measure**

D. **convert**

A. (speech) 1 ÷ 4 = .25

B. (thought) 75% of 10 = 7.5

C. (thought) 3 inches

D. (thought) 1 mi. = 1.6 km

(sign) 1 MILE TO LAKE

Fractions and Decimals

1. one whole
   1 = 1.00

2. one half
   1/2 = .5

3. one third
   1/3 = .333

4. one fourth
   1/4 = .25

5. one eighth
   1/8 = .125

Percents

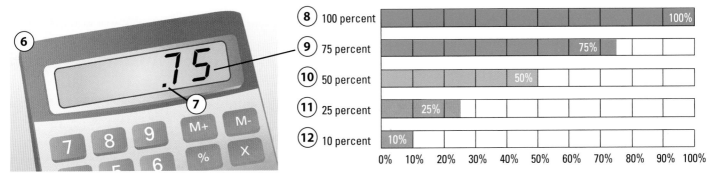

6. calculator

7. decimal point

8. 100 percent — 100%

9. 75 percent — 75%

10. 50 percent — 50%

11. 25 percent — 25%

12. 10 percent — 10%

Measurement

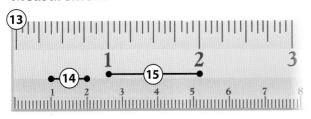

13. ruler

14. centimeter [cm]

15. inch [in.]

Dimensions

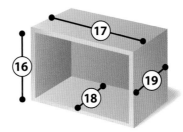

16. height

17. length

18. depth

19. width

Equivalencies

12 inches = 1 foot	
3 feet = 1 yard	
1,760 yards = 1 mile	
1 inch = 2.54 centimeters	
1 yard = .91 meter	
1 mile = 1.6 kilometers	

Telling Time

1. hour
2. minutes
3. seconds
4. a.m.
5. p.m.

6. 1:00
one o'clock

7. 1:05
one-oh-five
five after one

8. 1:10
one-ten
ten after one

9. 1:15
one-fifteen
a quarter after one

10. 1:20
one-twenty
twenty after one

11. 1:30
one-thirty
half past one

12. 1:40
one-forty
twenty to two

13. 1:45
one-forty-five
a quarter to two

Times of Day

14. sunrise
15. morning
16. noon
17. afternoon

18. sunset
19. evening
20. night
21. midnight

Ways to talk about time

I wake up at 6:30 a.m.
I wake up at 6:30 in the morning.
I wake up at 6:30.

Pair practice. Make new conversations.

A: *What time do you wake up on weekdays?*
B: *At 6:30 a.m. How about you?*
A: *I wake up at 7:00.*

22. early

23. on time

24. late

25. daylight saving time

26. standard time

Time Zones

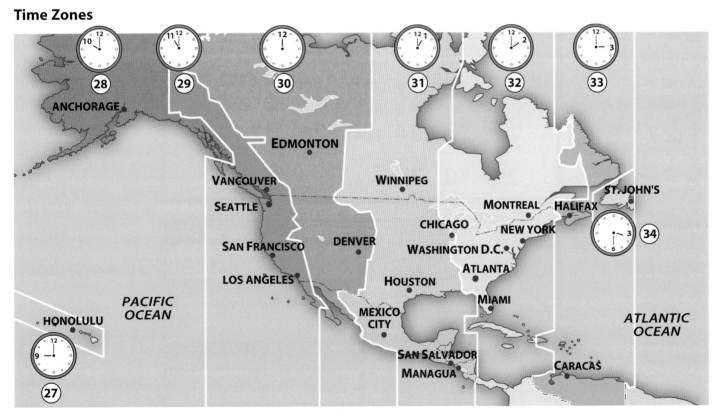

27. Hawaii-Aleutian time

28. Alaska time

29. Pacific time

30. Mountain time

31. Central time

32. Eastern time

33. Atlantic time

34. Newfoundland time

Survey your class. Record the responses.

1. When do you watch television? study? relax?

2. Do you like to stay up after midnight?

Report: *Most of us… Some of us…*

Think about it. Discuss.

1. What is your favorite time of day? Why?

2. Do you think daylight saving time is a good idea?

3. What's good about staying up after midnight?

The Calendar

1. date
2. day
3. month
4. year

5. today
6. tomorrow
7. yesterday

Days of the Week

8. Sunday
9. Monday
10. Tuesday
11. Wednesday
12. Thursday
13. Friday
14. Saturday

15. week
16. weekdays
17. weekend

SUN	MON	TUE	WED	THU	FRI	SAT
1	2	3	4	5	6	7
8	9	10	11	12	13	14
15	16	17	18	19	20	21
22	23	24	25	26	27	28
29	30	31				

Frequency

18. last week
19. this week
20. next week

21. every day / daily
22. once a week
23. twice a week
24. three times a week

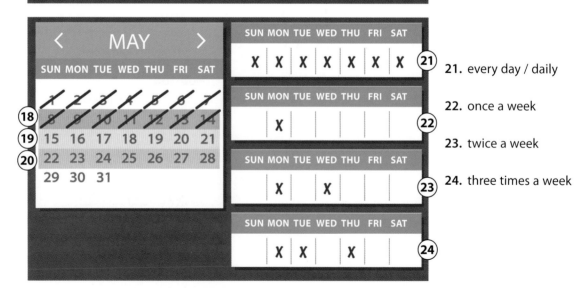

Ways to say the date

Today is <u>May 10th</u>. It's the <u>tenth</u>.
Yesterday was <u>May 9th</u>.
The party is on <u>May 21st</u>.

Pair practice. Make new conversations.

A: *The <u>test</u> is on <u>Friday</u>, <u>June 14th</u>.*
B: *Did you say <u>Friday</u>, the <u>fourteenth</u>?*
A: *Yes, the <u>fourteenth</u>.*

25. JAN

SUN	MON	TUE	WED	THU	FRI	SAT
						1
2	3	4	5	6	7	8
9	10	11	12	13	14	15
16	17	18	19	20	21	22
23	24	25	26	27	28	29
30	31					

26. FEB

SUN	MON	TUE	WED	THU	FRI	SAT
	1	2	3	4	5	
6	7	8	9	10	11	12
13	14	15	16	17	18	19
20	21	22	23	24	25	26
27	28					

27. MAR

SUN	MON	TUE	WED	THU	FRI	SAT
	1	2	3	4	5	
6	7	8	9	10	11	12
13	14	15	16	17	18	19
20	21	22	23	24	25	26
27	28	29	30	31		

28. APR

SUN	MON	TUE	WED	THU	FRI	SAT
					1	2
3	4	5	6	7	8	9
10	11	12	13	14	15	16
17	18	19	20	21	22	23
24	25	26	27	28	29	30

29. MAY

SUN	MON	TUE	WED	THU	FRI	SAT
1	2	3	4	5	6	7
8	9	10	11	12	13	14
15	16	17	18	19	20	21
22	23	24	25	26	27	28
29	30	31				

30. JUN

SUN	MON	TUE	WED	THU	FRI	SAT
			1	2	3	4
5	6	7	8	9	10	11
12	13	14	15	16	17	18
19	20	21	22	23	24	25
26	27	28	29	30		

31. JUL

SUN	MON	TUE	WED	THU	FRI	SAT
					1	2
3	4	5	6	7	8	9
10	11	12	13	14	15	16
17	18	19	20	21	22	23
24	25	26	27	28	29	30
31						

32. AUG

SUN	MON	TUE	WED	THU	FRI	SAT
	1	2	3	4	5	6
7	8	9	10	11	12	13
14	15	16	17	18	19	20
21	22	23	24	25	26	27
28	29	30	31			

33. SEP

SUN	MON	TUE	WED	THU	FRI	SAT
				1	2	3
4	5	6	7	8	9	10
11	12	13	14	15	16	17
18	19	20	21	22	23	24
25	26	27	28	29	30	

34. OCT

SUN	MON	TUE	WED	THU	FRI	SAT
						1
2	3	4	5	6	7	8
9	10	11	12	13	14	15
16	17	18	19	20	21	22
23	24	25	26	27	28	29
30	31					

35. NOV

SUN	MON	TUE	WED	THU	FRI	SAT
	1	2	3	4	5	
6	7	8	9	10	11	12
13	14	15	16	17	18	19
20	21	22	23	24	25	26
27	28	29	30			

36. DEC

SUN	MON	TUE	WED	THU	FRI	SAT
				1	2	3
4	5	6	7	8	9	10
11	12	13	14	15	16	17
18	19	20	21	22	23	24
25	26	27	28	29	30	31

Months of the Year

25. January

26. February

27. March

28. April

29. May

30. June

31. July

32. August

33. September

34. October

35. November

36. December

Seasons

37. spring

38. summer

39. fall / autumn

40. winter

Dictate to your partner. Take turns.

A: *Write Monday.*
B: *Is it spelled M-o-n-d-a-y?*
A: *Yes, that's right.*

Survey your class. Record the responses.

1. What is the busiest day of your week?
2. What is your favorite day?
Report: *Ten of us said Monday is our busiest day.*

1. birthday

2. wedding

3. anniversary

4. appointment

5. parent-teacher conference

6. vacation

7. religious holiday

8. legal holiday

Legal Holidays

Happy New Year!

JAN 1

I have a dream.

JAN

FEB

MAY

JUL 4

SEP

PROUD TO WORK

OCT

NOV

NOV

DEC 25

9. New Year's Day

10. Martin Luther King Jr. Day

11. Presidents' Day

12. Memorial Day

13. Fourth of July / Independence Day

14. Labor Day

15. Columbus Day

16. Veterans Day

17. Thanksgiving

18. Christmas

Pair practice. Make new conversations.

A: *When is your <u>birthday</u>?*
B: *It's on <u>January 31st</u>. How about yours?*
A: *It's on <u>December 22nd</u>.*

Internet Research: independence day

Type "independence day, world" in the search bar.
Report: *<u>Peru</u> celebrates its independence on <u>7/28</u>.*

1. **little** hand
2. **big** hand

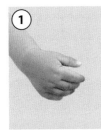 

13. **heavy** box
14. **light** box

 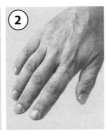

3. **fast** speed
4. **slow** speed

15. **same** color
16. **different** colors

5. **hard** chair
6. **soft** chair

17. **bad** news
18. **good** news

There was an earthquake.

Everyone is OK!

7. **thick** book
8. **thin** book

19. **expensive** ring
20. **cheap** ring

25¢

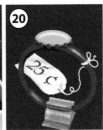 

9. **full** glass
10. **empty** glass

21. **beautiful** view
22. **ugly** view

11. **noisy** children / **loud** children
12. **quiet** children

23. **easy** problem
24. **difficult** problem / **hard** problem

$$1 + 1 = 2$$

$$x^2 - 22\tfrac{1}{2}x = -8\tfrac{1}{3}x^2 - 11\tfrac{2}{3}$$

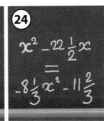 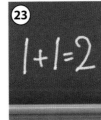

Survey your class. Record the responses.

1. Are you a slow walker or a fast walker?
2. Do you prefer loud parties or quiet parties?

Report: *Five of us prefer quiet parties.*

Use the new words.

Look at pages 154–155. Describe the things you see.

A: *The subway is full.*
B: *The motorcycle is noisy.*

23

Basic Colors

1. red

2. yellow

3. blue

4. orange

5. green

6. purple

7. pink

8. violet

9. turquoise

10. dark blue

11. light blue

12. bright blue

Neutral Colors

13. black

14. white

15. gray

16. cream / ivory

17. brown

18. beige / tan

Survey your class. Record the responses.

1. What colors are you wearing today?
2. What colors do you like? What colors do you dislike?
Report: *Most of us… Some of us…*

Use the new words. Look at pages 86–87.
Take turns naming the colors you see.

A: *His shirt is <u>blue</u>.*
B: *Her shoes are <u>white</u>.*

1. The yellow sweaters are **on the left**.

2. The purple sweaters are **in the middle**.

3. The brown sweaters are **on the right**.

4. The red sweaters are **above** the blue sweaters.

5. The blue sweaters are **below** the red sweaters.

6. The turquoise sweater is **in** the box.

7. The white sweater is **in front of** the black sweater.

8. The black sweater is **behind** the white sweater.

9. The violet sweater is **next to** the gray sweater.

10. The gray sweater is **under** the orange sweater.

11. The orange sweater is **on** the gray sweater.

12. The green sweater is **between** the pink sweaters.

More vocabulary	**Role play. Make new conversations.**
near: in the same area **far from:** not near	A: *Excuse me. Where are the <u>red</u> sweaters?* B: *They're <u>on the left</u>, <u>above</u> the <u>blue</u> sweaters.* A: *Thanks very much.*

25

Coins

1. $.01 = 1¢
a penny / 1 cent

3. $.10 = 10¢
a dime / 10 cents

5. $.50 = 50¢
a half dollar

2. $.05 = 5¢
a nickel / 5 cents

4. $.25 = 25¢
a quarter / 25 cents

6. $1.00
a dollar coin

Bills

7. $1.00
a dollar

8. $5.00
five dollars

9. $10.00
ten dollars

10. $20.00
twenty dollars

11. $50.00
fifty dollars

12. $100.00
one hundred dollars

A. Get change.

B. Borrow money.

C. Lend money.

D. Pay back the money.

Pair practice. Make new conversations.

A: *Do you have change for a dollar?*
B: *Sure. How about two quarters and five dimes?*
A: *Perfect!*

Identify Mark's problem. Brainstorm solutions.

Mark doesn't like to lend money. His boss, Lia, asks, "Can I borrow $20.00?" What can Mark say? What will Lia say?

Ways to Pay

A. pay cash

B. use a credit card

C. use a debit card

D. write a (personal) check

E. use a gift card

F. cash a traveler's check

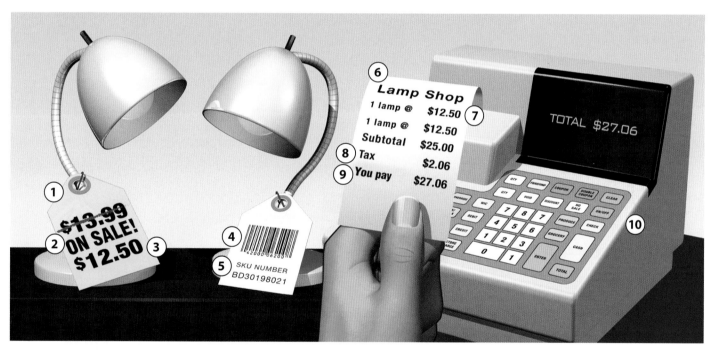

Lamp Shop
1 lamp @	$12.50
1 lamp @	$12.50
Subtotal	$25.00
Tax	$2.06
You pay	$27.06

TOTAL $27.06

$13.99 ON SALE! $12.50

SKU NUMBER
BD30198021

1. price tag	3. sale price	5. SKU number	7. price / cost	9. total
2. regular price	4. bar code	6. receipt	8. sales tax	10. cash register

G. buy / pay for

H. return

I. exchange

27

Same and Different

1. twins
2. sweater
3. matching
4. disappointed
5. navy blue
6. happy

A. **shop**
B. **keep**

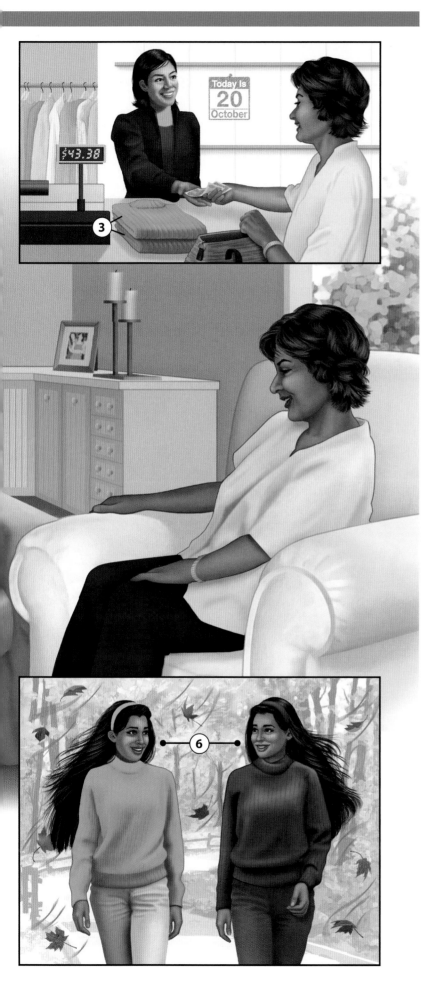

What do you see in the pictures?

1. Who is the woman shopping for?
2. Does she buy matching sweaters or different sweaters?
3. How does Anya feel about her green sweater? What does she do?
4. What does Manda do with her sweater?

Read the story.

Same and Different

Mrs. Kumar likes to <u>shop</u> for her <u>twins</u>. Today she's looking at <u>sweaters</u>. There are many different colors on sale. Mrs. Kumar chooses two <u>matching</u> green sweaters.

The next day, Manda and Anya open their gifts. Manda likes the green sweater, but Anya is <u>disappointed</u>. Mrs. Kumar understands the problem. Anya wants to be different.

Manda <u>keeps</u> her sweater, but Anya goes to the store. She exchanges her green sweater for a <u>navy blue</u> sweater. It's an easy answer to Anya's problem. Now the twins can be warm, <u>happy</u>, and different.

Reread the story.

1. Underline the last sentence in each paragraph. Why are these sentences important?
2. Retell the story in your own words.

What do you think?

3. Imagine you are Anya. Would you keep the sweater or exchange it? Why?

Adults and Children

1. man
2. woman
3. women
4. men
5. senior citizen

Listen and point. Take turns.

A: *Point to a woman.*
B: *Point to a senior citizen.*
A: *Point to an infant.*

Dictate to your partner. Take turns.

A: *Write woman.*
B: *Is that spelled w-o-m-a-n?*
A: *Yes, that's right, woman.*

30

Ways to talk about age

1 month–3 months old = **infant**	13–19 years old = **teenager**
18 months–3 years old = **toddler**	18+ years old = **adult**
3 years old–12 years old = **child**	62+ years old = **senior citizen**

Pair practice. Make new conversations.

A: *How old is <u>Sandra</u>?*

B: *<u>She's 13</u> years old.*

A: *Wow, <u>she's a teenager</u> now!*

31

Describing People

Age

1. young

2. middle-aged

3. elderly

Height

4. tall

5. average height

6. short

Weight

7. heavy / fat

8. average weight

9. thin / slender

Disabilities

10. physically challenged

11. sight impaired / blind

12. hearing impaired / deaf

Appearance

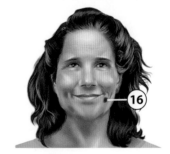

13. attractive   14. cute   15. pregnant   16. mole   17. pierced ear

18. tattoo

Ways to describe people

He's a <u>heavy</u>, <u>young</u> man.
She's a <u>pregnant</u> woman with <u>a mole</u>.
He's <u>sight impaired</u>.

Use the new words.

Look at pages 44-45. Describe the people you see. Take turns.

A: *This <u>elderly</u> woman is <u>short</u> and a little <u>heavy</u>.*
B: *This <u>young</u> man is <u>physically challenged</u>.*

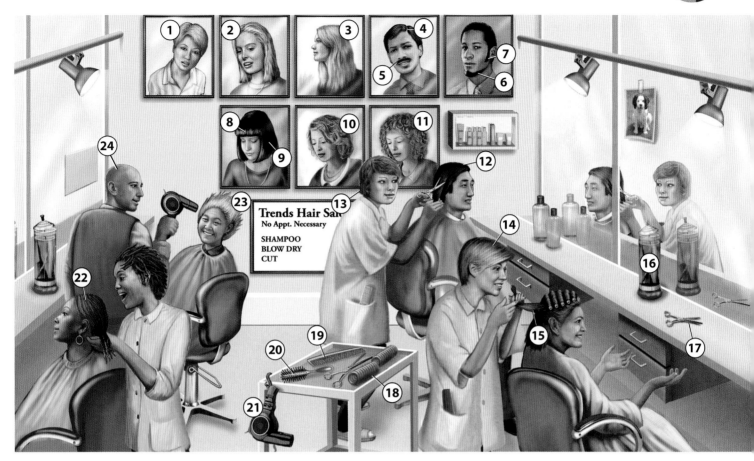

1. short hair	**6.** beard	**11.** curly hair	**16.** sanitizing jar	**21.** blow dryer
2. shoulder-length hair	**7.** sideburns	**12.** black hair	**17.** shears	**22.** cornrows
3. long hair	**8.** bangs	**13.** red hair	**18.** rollers	**23.** gray hair
4. part	**9.** straight hair	**14.** blond hair	**19.** comb	**24.** bald
5. mustache	**10.** wavy hair	**15.** brown hair	**20.** brush	

Style Hair

A. **cut** hair

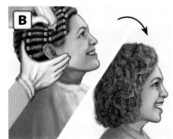

B. **perm** hair

C. **add** highlights

D. **color** hair / **dye** hair

Ways to talk about hair

Describe hair in this order: length, style, and then color.

She has <u>long</u>, <u>straight</u>, <u>brown</u> hair.

Role play. Talk to a stylist.

A: *I need a new hairstyle.*

B: *How about <u>short</u> and <u>straight</u>?*

A: *Great. Do you think I should <u>dye</u> it?*

33

Families

1. grandmother
2. grandfather
3. mother
4. father
5. sister
6. brother
7. aunt
8. uncle
9. cousin

Tim Lee's Family

GRANDPARENTS

Immediate Family

1. Min
2. Lu

PARENTS

3. Rose
4. Ken
7. Lynn
8. Dan

CHILDREN

Tim
5. Lily
6. Alex
9. Emily

10. mother-in-law
11. father-in-law
12. wife
13. husband
14. daughter
15. son
16. sister-in-law
17. brother-in-law
18. niece
19. nephew

Ana Garcia's Family

Extended Family

10. Eva
11. Sam

12. Ana
13. Tito
16. Marta
17. Carlos

14. Sara
15. Felix
18. Alice
19. Eddie

More vocabulary

Tim is Min and Lu's **grandson**.
Lily and Emily are Min and Lu's **granddaughters**.
Alex is Min's youngest **grandchild**.

Ana is Eva and Sam's **daughter-in-law**.
Carlos is Eva and Sam's **son-in-law**.
Note: Ana's married. = Ana **is** married.
Ana's **husband** = the man married to Ana

20. married couple

21. divorced couple

22. single mother

23. single father

Carol, Bruce, and Lisa

Lisa, Age 4

Lisa Green's Family

Lisa, Age 7

Rick

Carol

Bruce

Sue

Lisa, Today

Mary

David

Kim

Bill

24. remarried

25. stepfather

26. stepmother

27. half sister

28. half brother

29. stepsister

30. stepbrother

More vocabulary

Bruce is Carol's **former husband** or **ex-husband**.
Carol is Bruce's **former wife** or **ex-wife**.
Lisa is the **stepdaughter** of both Rick and Sue.

Use the new words.
Ask and answer questions about Lisa's family.

A: Who is _Lisa's_ _half sister_?
B: _Mary_ is. Who is _Lisa's_ _stepsister_?

A. hold

B. nurse

C. feed

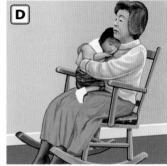

D. rock

E. undress

F. bathe

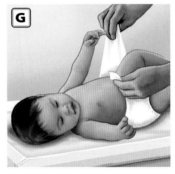

G. change a diaper

H. dress

I. comfort

Good job!

J. praise

No!

K. discipline

L. buckle up

M. play with

N. read to

O. sing a lullaby

P. kiss goodnight

Look at the pictures.
Describe what is happening.

A: *She's changing her baby's diaper.*
B: *He's kissing his son goodnight.*

Talk about your experience.

I am great at playing with toddlers.
I have a lot of experience changing diapers.
I know how to hold an infant.

36

1. bottle	**5.** bib	**9.** safety pins	**13.** baby lotion
2. nipple	**6.** high chair	**10.** disposable diaper	**14.** baby powder
3. formula	**7.** diaper pail	**11.** diaper bag	**15.** potty seat
4. baby food	**8.** cloth diaper	**12.** wipes	**16.** training pants

17. baby carrier	**20.** car safety seat	**23.** nursery rhymes	**26.** teething ring
18. stroller	**21.** booster car seat	**24.** teddy bear	**27.** rattle
19. carriage	**22.** rocking chair	**25.** pacifier	**28.** night light

Dictate to your partner. Take turns.

A: *Write pacifier.*
B: *Was that pacifier, p-a-c-i-f-i-e-r?*
A: *Yes, that's right.*

Think about it. Discuss.

1. How can parents discipline toddlers? teens?
2. What are some things you can say to praise a child?
3. Why are nursery rhymes important for young children?

A. wake up

B. get up

C. take a shower

D. get dressed

E. eat breakfast

F. make lunch

G. take the children to school /
drop off the kids

H. take the bus to school

I. **drive** to work / **go** to work

J. be in class

K. work

L. go to the grocery store

M. pick up the kids

N. leave work

Grammar Point: third-person singular

For *he* and *she*, add **-s** or **-es** to the verb:
He eats breakfast.   *He watches TV.*
She makes lunch.   *She goes to the store.*

For two-part verbs, put the **-s** on the first part: wake**s** up, drop**s** off.
Be and *have* are different (irregular).
*He **is** in bed at 5 a.m. He **has** breakfast at 7 a.m.*

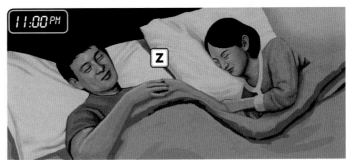

O. **clean** the house

P. **exercise**

Q. **cook** dinner / **make** dinner

R. **come** home / **get** home

S. **have** dinner / **eat** dinner

T. **do** homework

U. **relax**

V. **read** the paper

W. **check** email

X. **watch** TV

Y. **go** to bed

Z. **go** to sleep

Pair practice. Make new conversations.

A: *When does he go to work?*
B: *He goes to work at 8:00 a.m. When does she make dinner?*
A: *She makes dinner at 6:00 p.m.*

Internet Research: housework

Type "time survey, chart, housework" in the search bar.
Report: *According to the survey, men prepare food 17 minutes a day.*

39

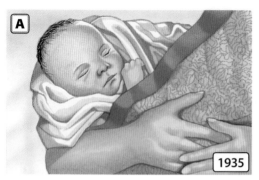

1935

A. **be born**

1940

B. **start** school

1. birth certificate

1950

C. **immigrate**

1953

D. **graduate**

2. Resident Alien card / green card

3. diploma

1953

E. **learn** to drive

1954

F. **get** a job

4. driver's license

1954

G. **become** a citizen

1955

H. **fall in love**

5. Social Security card

6. Certificate of Naturalization

Grammar Point: past tense

start					
learn	} + **ed**	immigrate	retire	}	
travel		graduate	die	} + **d**	

These verbs are different (irregular):

be – was	go – went	buy – bought
get – got	have – had	
become – became	fall – fell	

I. **go** to college — 1956

J. **get** engaged — 1958

7. college degree

K. **get** married — 1959

L. **have** a baby — 1961

8. marriage license

M. **buy** a home — 1965

N. **become** a grandparent — 1986

9. deed

O. **retire** — 2000

P. **travel** — 2005

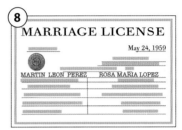

10. passport

Q. **volunteer** — 2006

R. **die** — 2008

11. death certificate

More vocabulary

When a husband dies, his wife becomes a **widow**.
When a wife dies, her husband becomes a **widower**.
Someone who is not living is **dead** or **deceased**.

Survey your class. Record the responses.

1. When did you start school? immigrate? learn to drive?
2. Do you want to become a citizen? travel? retire?
Report: *Most of us… Some of us…*

Feelings

1. hot
2. thirsty
3. sleepy
4. cold
5. hungry
6. full / satisfied

7. disgusted
8. calm
9. uncomfortable
10. nervous

11. in pain
12. sick
13. worried
14. well
15. relieved

16. hurt
17. lonely
18. in love

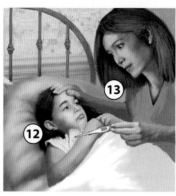

Pair practice. Make new conversations.

A: *How are you doing?*
B: *I'm <u>hungry</u>. How about you?*
A: *I'm <u>hungry</u> and <u>thirsty</u>, too!*

Use the new words.
Look at pages 40–41. Describe what each person is feeling.

A: *Martin is <u>excited</u>.*
B: *Martin's mother is <u>proud</u>.*

 19. sad

 20. homesick

 21. proud

 22. excited

 23. scared / afraid

 24. embarrassed

 25. bored

 26. confused

 27. frustrated

 28. upset

29. angry

 30. surprised

 31. happy

 32. tired

---

Identify Kenge's problem. Brainstorm solutions.

Kenge wants to learn English quickly, but it's difficult.
He makes a lot of mistakes and gets frustrated.
And he's homesick, too. What can he do?

More vocabulary

exhausted: very tired
furious: very angry
humiliated: very embarrassed

overjoyed: very happy
starving: very hungry
terrified: very scared

A Family Reunion

1. banner
2. baseball game
3. opinion
4. balloons
5. glad
6. relatives
A. **laugh**
B. **misbehave**

I think large families are best.

What do you see in the picture?

1. How many relatives are there at this reunion?

2. How many children are there? Which children are misbehaving?

3. What are people doing at this reunion?

Read the story.

A Family Reunion

Ben Lu has a lot of <u>relatives</u> and they're all at his house. Today is the Lu family reunion.

There is a lot of good food. There are also <u>balloons</u> and a <u>banner</u>. And this year there are four new babies!

People are having a good time at the reunion. Ben's grandfather and his aunt are talking about the <u>baseball game</u>. His cousins <u>are laughing</u>. His mother-in-law is giving her <u>opinion</u>. And many of the children <u>are misbehaving</u>.

Ben looks at his family and smiles. He loves his relatives, but he's <u>glad</u> the reunion is once a year.

Reread the story.

1. Find this sentence in the story: "He loves his relatives, but he's glad the reunion is once a year." Explain what this sentence means.

2. Retell the story in your own words.

What do you think?

3. You are at Ben's party. You see a child misbehave. No other guests see him. What do you do? What do you say?

45

The Home

1. yard

2. roof

3. bedroom

4. door

5. bathroom

6. kitchen

7. floor

8. dining area

Listen and point. Take turns.

A: *Point to <u>the kitchen</u>.*
B: *Point to <u>the living room</u>.*
A: *Point to <u>the basement</u>.*

Dictate to your partner. Take turns.

A: *Write <u>kitchen</u>.*
B: *Was that <u>k-i-t-c-h-e-n</u>?*
A: *Yes, that's right, <u>kitchen</u>.*

9. attic

10. kids' bedroom

11. baby's room / nursery

12. window

13. living room

14. basement

15. garage

Ways to give locations

I'm **at** home.
I'm **in** the kitchen.
I'm **on** the roof.

It's **in** the laundry room.
It's **on** the floor.

Pair practice. Ask and answer questions.

A: *Where's the <u>man</u>?*
B: <u>*He's*</u> *in the <u>attic</u>. Where's the <u>mother</u>?*
A: <u>*She's*</u> *in the <u>living room</u>.*

47

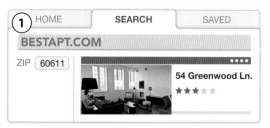

1. apartment search tool

2. listing / classified ad

Abbreviations

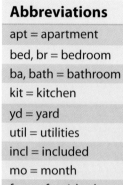

apt = apartment
bed, br = bedroom
ba, bath = bathroom
kit = kitchen
yd = yard
util = utilities
incl = included
mo = month
furn = furnished
unfurn = unfurnished
mgr = manager
eves = evenings
AC = air conditioning

3. furnished apartment

4. unfurnished apartment

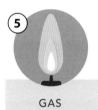    

GAS WATER ELECTRICITY TRASH COLLECTION CABLE INTERNET ACCESS

5. utilities

Renting an Apartment

A. Call the manager.

Are utilities included?

No, they aren't.

B. Ask about the features.

C. Submit an application.

D. Sign the rental agreement.

E. Pay the first and last month's rent.

F. Move in.

More vocabulary

lease: a monthly or yearly rental agreement
redecorate: to change the paint and furniture in a home
move out: to pack and leave a home

Survey your class. Record the responses.

1. What features do you look for in a home?
2. How did you find your current home?
Report: *Most of us… Some of us…*

Buying a House

G. **Meet** with a realtor.

H. **Look** at houses.

I. **Make** an offer.

J. **Get** a loan.

K. **Take** ownership.

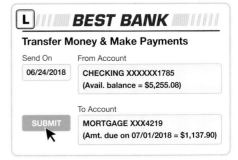

L. **Make** a mortgage payment.

Moving In

M. **Pack**.

N. **Unpack**.

O. **Put** the utilities in your name.

P. **Paint**.

Q. **Arrange** the furniture.

R. **Meet** the neighbors.

Ways to ask about a home's features

Are <u>utilities</u> included?
Is <u>the kitchen</u> large and sunny?
Are <u>the neighbors</u> quiet?

Role play. Talk to an apartment manager.

A: *Hi. I'm calling about <u>the apartment</u>.*
B: *OK. It's <u>unfurnished</u> and rent is $<u>800</u> a month.*
A: *<u>Are utilities included</u>?*

Apartments

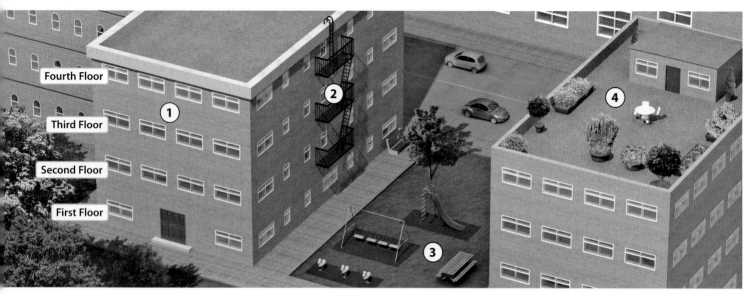

Fourth Floor

Third Floor

Second Floor

First Floor

1. apartment building
2. fire escape
3. playground
4. roof garden

Entrance

Apartment Available
2BR + 2BA
555-4263

5. intercom / speaker
7. vacancy sign

6. tenant
8. manager / superintendent

Lobby

9. elevator
11. mailboxes

10. stairs / stairway

Basement

SOAP SOFTENER

LAUNDRY ROOM

RECREATION ROOM

GARAGE

12. washer
14. big-screen TV
16. security gate
18. parking space

13. dryer
15. pool table
17. storage locker
19. security camera

Grammar Point: *Is there...? / Are there...?*

Is there a rec room?   ***Are there*** stairs?
Yes, there is.   Yes, there are.
No, there isn't.   No, there aren't.

Look at the pictures.
Describe the apartment building.

A: There's <u>a pool table</u> in <u>the recreation room</u>.
B: There **are** <u>parking spaces</u> in <u>the garage</u>.

50

APARTMENT COMPLEX

20. balcony

21. courtyard

22. swimming pool

23. trash bin

24. alley

Hallway

25. emergency exit

26. trash chute

Rental Office

27. landlord

28. lease / rental agreement

29. prospective tenant

An Apartment Entryway

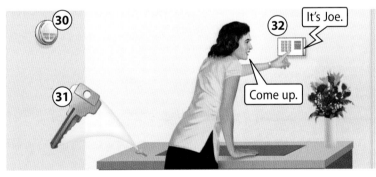

It's Joe.

Come up.

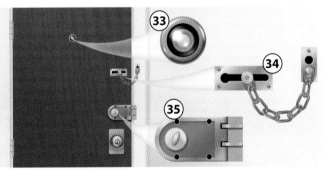

30. smoke detector

31. key

32. buzzer

33. peephole

34. door chain

35. deadbolt lock

More vocabulary

upstairs: the floor(s) above you
downstairs: the floor(s) below you
fire exit: another name for emergency exit

Role play. Talk to a landlord.

A: *Is there a swimming pool in this complex?*
B: *Yes, there is. It's near the courtyard.*
A: *Is there…?*

51

1. the city / an urban area **2.** the suburbs **3.** a small town / a village **4.** the country / a rural area

5. condominium / condo

6. townhouse

7. mobile home

8. college dormitory / dorm

9. farm

10. ranch

11. senior housing

12. nursing home

13. shelter

More vocabulary

co-op: an apartment building owned by residents
duplex: a house divided into two homes
two-story house: a house with two floors

Think about it. Discuss.

1. Compare life in a city and a small town.
2. Compare life in a city and the country.

52

Front Yard and House

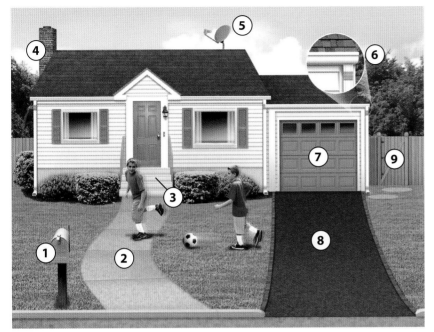

Front Porch

1. mailbox
2. front walk
3. steps

4. chimney
5. satellite dish
6. gutter

7. garage door
8. driveway
9. gate

10. storm door
11. front door
12. doorknob

13. porch light
14. doorbell
15. screen door

Backyard

16. patio
17. grill
18. sliding glass door

19. patio furniture
20. flower bed
21. hose

22. sprinkler
23. hammock
24. garbage can

25. compost pile
26. lawn
27. vegetable garden

A. **take** a nap
B. **garden**

A Kitchen

1. cabinet
2. shelf
3. paper towels
4. sink
5. dish rack
6. coffee maker
7. garbage disposal

8. dishwasher
9. refrigerator
10. freezer
11. toaster
12. blender
13. microwave
14. electric can opener

15. toaster oven
16. pot
17. teakettle
18. stove
19. burner
20. oven
21. broiler

22. counter
23. drawer
24. pan
25. electric mixer
26. food processor
27. cutting board
28. mixing bowl

Ways to talk about location using *on* and *in*

Use **on** for the counter, shelf, burner, stove, and cutting board. *It's on the counter.* Use **in** for the dishwasher, oven, sink, and drawer. *Put it in the sink.*

Pair practice. Make new conversations.

A: *Please move the blender.*
B: *Sure. Do you want it in the cabinet?*
A: *No, put it on the counter.*

lothes 1 and 2 with words

 pajamas

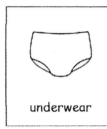 underwear

 pants

 dress

 socks

 shoes

 coat

 nightgown

 shorts

 shirt

 diaper

 zip

 snap

 sweater

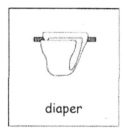 belt

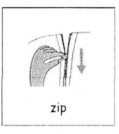 winter hat

 mittens

 boots

 bathing suit

 bathing suit

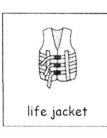 life jacket

 hat

 sandals

 wristwatch

show images with no words

1

2

3

4

5

6

7

1. dish / plate	7. coffee mug	13. salt and pepper shakers	19. fan
2. bowl	8. dining room chair	14. sugar bowl	20. platter
3. fork	9. dining room table	15. creamer	21. serving bowl
4. knife	10. napkin	16. teapot	22. hutch
5. spoon	11. placemat	17. tray	23. vase
6. teacup	12. tablecloth	18. light fixture	24. buffet

Ways to make requests at the table

May I have the sugar bowl?
Would you pass the creamer, please?
Could I have a coffee mug?

Role play. Request items at the table.

A: *What do you need?*
B: *Could I have a coffee mug?*
A: *Certainly. And would you…?*

55

1. love seat
2. throw pillow
3. basket
4. houseplant
5. entertainment center
6. TV (television)
7. digital video recorder (DVR)
8. stereo system
9. painting
10. wall
11. mantle
12. fire screen
13. fireplace
14. end table
15. floor lamp
16. drapes / curtains
17. window
18. sofa / couch
19. coffee table
20. candle
21. candle holder
22. armchair / easy chair
23. ottoman
24. carpet

More vocabulary

light bulb: the light inside a lamp
magazine rack: a piece of furniture for magazines
sofa cushions: the pillows that are part of the sofa

Internet Research: furniture prices

Type any furniture item and the word "price" in the search bar.
Report: *I found a sofa for $300.00.*

1. hamper	**8.** faucet	**15.** towel rack	**22.** medicine cabinet
2. bathtub	**9.** hot water	**16.** bath towel	**23.** toothbrush
3. soap dish	**10.** cold water	**17.** hand towel	**24.** toothbrush holder
4. soap	**11.** grab bar	**18.** mirror	**25.** sink
5. rubber mat	**12.** tile	**19.** toilet paper	**26.** wastebasket
6. washcloth	**13.** showerhead	**20.** toilet brush	**27.** scale
7. drain	**14.** shower curtain	**21.** toilet	**28.** bath mat

---

More vocabulary

stall shower: a shower without a bathtub
half bath: a bathroom with no shower or tub
linen closet: a closet for towels and sheets

Survey your class. Record the responses.

1. Is your toothbrush on the sink or in the medicine cabinet?
2. Do you have a bathtub or a shower?
Report: *Most of us… Some of us…*

1. dresser / bureau	8. mini-blinds	15. blanket	22. rug
2. drawer	9. bed	16. quilt	23. night table / nightstand
3. photos	10. headboard	17. dust ruffle	24. alarm clock
4. picture frame	11. pillow	18. bed frame	25. lamp
5. closet	12. fitted sheet	19. box spring	26. lampshade
6. full-length mirror	13. flat sheet	20. mattress	27. light switch
7. curtains	14. pillowcase	21. wood floor	28. outlet

Look at the pictures.
Describe the bedroom.

A: *There's a lamp on the nightstand*.
B: *There's a mirror in the closet*.

Survey your class. Record the responses.

1. Do you prefer a hard or a soft mattress?
2. How many pillows do you like on your bed?
Report: *All of us… A few of us…*

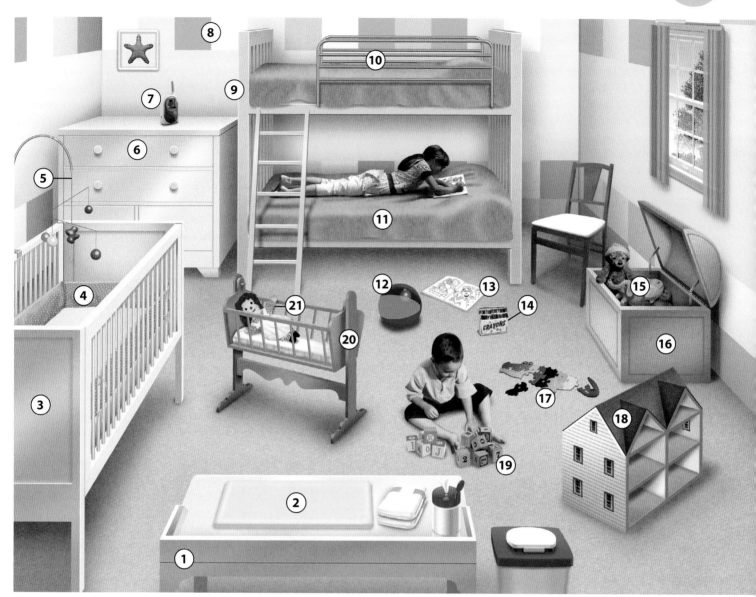

Furniture and Accessories

1. changing table
2. changing pad
3. crib
4. bumper pad
5. mobile
6. chest of drawers
7. baby monitor
8. wallpaper
9. bunk beds
10. safety rail
11. bedspread

Toys and Games

12. ball
13. coloring book
14. crayons
15. stuffed animals
16. toy chest
17. puzzle
18. dollhouse
19. blocks
20. cradle
21. doll

Pair practice. Make new conversations.

A: *Where's the <u>changing pad</u>?*
B: *It's on the <u>changing table</u>.*

Think about it. Discuss.

1. Which toys help children learn? How?
2. Which toys are good for older and younger children?
3. What safety features does this room need? Why?

Housework

A. **dust** the furniture

B. **recycle** the newspapers

C. **clean** the oven

D. **mop** the floor

E. **polish** the furniture

F. **make** the bed

G. **put away** the toys

H. **vacuum** the carpet

I. **wash** the windows

J. **sweep** the floor

K. **scrub** the sink

L. **empty** the trash

M. **wash** the dishes

N. **dry** the dishes

O. **wipe** the counter

P. **change** the sheets

Q. **take out** the garbage

Pair practice. Make new conversations.

A: *Let's clean this place. First, I'll* sweep the floor.
B: *I'll* mop the floor *when you finish.*
A: *OK. After that we can…*

Think about it. Discuss.

1. Rank housework tasks from difficult to easy.
2. Categorize housework tasks by age: children, teens, adults.

 1
 2
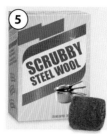 3
 4
 5
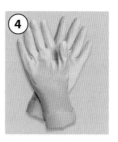 6

 7
 8
 9
 10
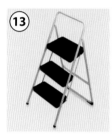 11
 12

 13
 14
 15
 16
 17
 18

 19
 20
 21
 22
 23
 24

1. feather duster
2. recycling bin
3. oven cleaner
4. rubber gloves
5. steel-wool soap pads
6. sponge mop
7. bucket / pail
8. furniture polish

9. cleaning cloths
10. vacuum cleaner
11. vacuum cleaner attachments
12. vacuum cleaner bag
13. stepladder
14. glass cleaner
15. squeegee
16. broom

17. dustpan
18. multipurpose cleaner
19. sponge
20. scrub brush
21. dishwashing liquid
22. dish towel
23. disinfectant wipes
24. trash bags

Ways to ask for something

Please hand me <u>the squeegee</u>.
Can you get me <u>the broom</u>?
I need <u>the sponge mop</u>.

Pair practice. Make new conversations.

A: *Please hand me <u>the sponge mop</u>.*
B: *Here you go. Do you need <u>the bucket</u>?*
A: *Yes, please. Can you get me <u>the rubber gloves</u>, too?*

61

1. The water heater is **not working**.

2. The power is **out**.

3. The roof is **leaking**.

4. The tile is **cracked**.

5. The window is **broken**.

6. The lock is **broken**.

7. The steps are **broken**.

8. roofer

9. electrician

10. repairperson

11. locksmith

12. carpenter

13. fuse box

14. gas meter

More vocabulary

fix: to repair something that is broken
pests: termites, fleas, rats, etc.
exterminate: to kill household pests

Pair practice. Make new conversations.

A: *The <u>faucet is leaking</u>.*
B: *I think I can fix it.*
A: *I think we should call <u>a plumber</u>.*

15. The furnace is **broken**.

16. The pipes are **frozen**.

17. The faucet is **dripping**.

18. The sink is **overflowing**.

19. The toilet is **stopped up**.

20. plumber

21. exterminator

22. termites

23. ants

24. bedbugs

25. fleas

26. cockroaches / roaches

27. rats

28. mice*

***Note:** one mouse, two mice

Ways to ask about repairs

How much will it cost?
When can you begin?
How long will it take?

Role play. Talk to a repairperson.

A: *Can you <u>fix the roof</u>?*
B: *Yes, but it will take <u>two weeks</u>.*
A: *How much will it cost?*

The Tenant Meeting

1. roommates
2. party
3. music
4. DJ
5. noise
6. irritated
7. rules
8. mess
9. invitation
A. **dance**

What do you see in the pictures?

1. What happened in apartment 2B? How many people were there?

2. How did the neighbor feel? Why?

3. What rules did they write at the tenant meeting?

4. What did the roommates do after the tenant meeting?

 Read the story.

The Tenant Meeting

Sally Lopez and Tina Green are <u>roommates</u>. They live in apartment 2B. One night they had a big <u>party</u> with <u>music</u> and a <u>DJ</u>. There was a <u>mess</u> in the hallway. Their neighbors were very unhappy. Mr. Clark in 2A was very <u>irritated</u>. He hates <u>noise</u>!

The next day there was a tenant meeting. Everyone wanted <u>rules</u> about parties and loud music. The girls were very embarrassed.

After the meeting, the girls cleaned the mess in the hallway. Then they gave each neighbor an <u>invitation</u> to a new party. Everyone had a good time at the rec room party. Now the tenants have two new rules and a new place to <u>dance</u>.

Reread the story.

1. Find the word "irritated" in paragraph 1. What does it mean in this story?

2. Retell the story in your own words.

What do you think?

3. Imagine you are the neighbor in 2A. What do you say to Tina and Sally?

4. What are the most important rules in an apartment building? Why?

65

Back from the Market

1. fish

2. meat

3. chicken

4. cheese

5. milk

6. butter

7. eggs

8. vegetables

Listen and point. Take turns.

A: *Point to the vegetables.*
B: *Point to the bread.*
A: *Point to the fruit.*

Dictate to your partner. Take turns.

A: *Write vegetables.*
B: *Please spell vegetables for me.*
A: *V-e-g-e-t-a-b-l-e-s.*

9. fruit

10. rice

11. bread

12. pasta

13. grocery bag / shopping bag

14. shopping list

15. coupons

Ways to talk about food.

Do we need <u>eggs</u>?

Do we have any <u>pasta</u>?

We have some <u>vegetables</u>, but we need <u>fruit</u>.

Role play. Talk about your shopping list.

A: *Do we need <u>eggs</u>?*

B: *No, we have some.*

A: *Do we have any…?*

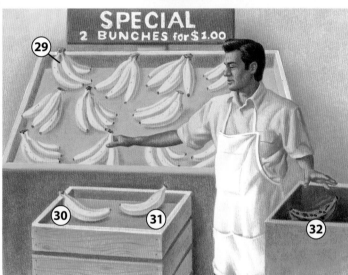

1. apples	9. tangerines	17. blackberries	25. raisins
2. bananas	10. peaches	18. watermelons	26. prunes
3. grapes	11. cherries	19. melons	27. figs
4. pears	12. apricots	20. papayas	28. dates
5. oranges	13. plums	21. mangoes	29. a bunch of bananas
6. grapefruit	14. strawberries	22. kiwi	30. **ripe** banana
7. lemons	15. raspberries	23. pineapples	31. **unripe** banana
8. limes	16. blueberries	24. coconuts	32. **rotten** banana

Pair practice. Make new conversations.

A: *What's your favorite fruit?*
B: *I like apples. Do you?*
A: *I prefer bananas.*

Survey your class. Record the responses.

1. What kinds of fruit are common in your native country?
2. What kinds of fruit are uncommon?
Report: *According to Luis, papayas are common in Peru.*

1. lettuce	9. celery	17. potatoes	25. zucchini
2. cabbage	10. cucumbers	18. sweet potatoes	26. asparagus
3. carrots	11. spinach	19. onions	27. mushrooms
4. radishes	12. corn	20. green onions / scallions	28. parsley
5. beets	13. broccoli	21. peas	29. chili peppers
6. tomatoes	14. cauliflower	22. artichokes	30. garlic
7. bell peppers	15. bok choy	23. eggplants	31. a **bag of** lettuce
8. string beans	16. turnips	24. squash	32. a **head of** lettuce

Pair practice. Make new conversations.

A: *Do you eat <u>broccoli</u>?*
B: *Yes. I like most vegetables, but not <u>peppers</u>.*
A: *Really? Well, I don't like <u>cauliflower</u>.*

Survey your class. Record the responses.

1. Which vegetables do you prefer to eat raw?
2. Which vegetables do you prefer to eat cooked?
Report: ____ of us prefer <u>raw carrots</u>. ____ of us prefer <u>cooked carrots</u>.

69

Meat and Poultry

MEAT

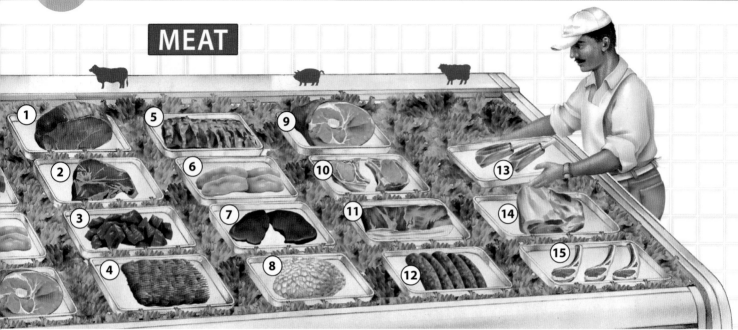

Beef

1. roast
2. steak
3. stewing beef
4. ground beef
5. beef ribs
6. veal cutlets
7. liver
8. tripe

Pork

9. ham
10. pork chops
11. bacon
12. sausage

Lamb

13. lamb shanks
14. leg of lamb
15. lamb chops

POULTRY

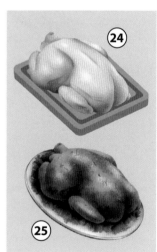

Poultry

16. chicken
17. turkey
18. duck
19. breasts
20. wings
21. legs
22. thighs
23. drumsticks
24. **raw** turkey
25. **cooked** turkey

More vocabulary

boneless: meat and poultry without bones
skinless: poultry without skin
vegetarian: a person who doesn't eat meat

Ways to ask about meat prices

*How much **is** that <u>roast</u>?*
*How much **are** those <u>cutlets</u>?*
*How much **is** the <u>ground beef</u>?*

Fish

1. trout

2. catfish

3. whole salmon

4. salmon steak

5. swordfish

6. halibut steak

7. tuna

8. cod

Shellfish

9. crab

10. lobster

11. shrimp

12. scallops

13. mussels

14. oysters

15. clams

16. fresh fish

17. frozen fish

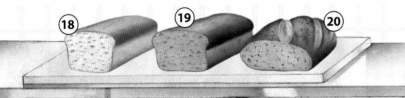

18. white bread

19. wheat bread

20. rye bread

21. roast beef

22. corned beef

23. pastrami

24. salami

25. smoked turkey

26. American cheese

27. Swiss cheese

28. cheddar cheese

29. mozzarella cheese

Ways to order at the counter

I'd like some <u>roast beef</u>.
I'll have <u>a halibut steak</u> and some <u>shrimp</u>.
Could I get some <u>Swiss cheese</u>?

Pair practice. Make new conversations.

A: *What can I get for you?*
B: *<u>I'd like some roast beef</u>. How about a pound?*
A: *A pound of <u>roast beef</u> coming up!*

71

A Grocery Store

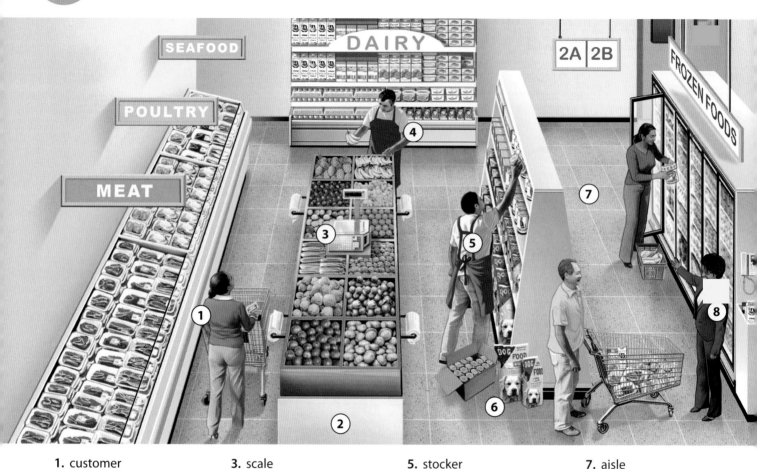

1. customer	3. scale	5. stocker	7. aisle
2. produce section	4. grocery clerk	6. pet food	8. manager

Canned Foods

17. beans
18. soup
19. tuna

Dairy

20. margarine
21. sour cream
22. yogurt

Grocery Products

23. aluminum foil
24. plastic wrap
25. plastic storage bags

Frozen Foods

26. ice cream
27. frozen vegetables
28. frozen dinner

Ways to ask for information in a grocery store

Excuse me, where are <u>the carrots</u>?
Can you please tell me where to find <u>the dog food</u>?
Do you have any <u>lamb chops</u> today?

Pair practice. Make new conversations.

A: <u>Can you please tell me where to find the dog food</u>?
B: *Sure. It's in <u>aisle 1B</u>. Do you need anything else?*
A: *Yes, where are <u>the carrots</u>?*

9. shopping basket

10. self-checkout

11. line

12. cart

13. checkstand

14. cashier / checker

15. bagger

16. cash register

Baking Products

29. flour

30. sugar

31. oil

Beverages

32. apple juice

33. coffee

34. soda / pop

Snack Foods

35. potato chips

36. nuts

37. candy bar

Baked Goods

38. cookies

39. cake

40. bagels

Survey your class. Record the responses.

1. What is your favorite grocery store?
2. Do you prefer to shop alone or with someone?

Report: *Most of us… Some of us…*

Think about it. Discuss.

1. Compare small grocery stores and large supermarkets.
2. Categorize the foods on this page as healthy or unhealthy. Explain your answers.

Containers and Packaging

 **1.** bottles

 2. jars

 **3.** cans

 **4.** cartons

 **5.** containers

 **6.** boxes

 **7.** bags

 **8.** packages

 **9.** six-packs

 **10.** loaves

 **11.** rolls

 **12.** tubes

 **13.** a bottle of water

  **14.** a jar of jam

 **15.** a can of beans

 **16.** a carton of eggs

 **17.** a container of cottage cheese

 **18.** a box of cereal

 **19.** a bag of flour

 **20.** a package of cookies

 **21.** a six-pack of soda (pop)

22. a loaf of bread

 **23.** a roll of paper towels

24. a tube of toothpaste

Grammar Point: count and noncount

Some foods can be counted: *an apple, two apples*.
Some foods can't be counted: *some rice, some water*.
For noncount foods, count containers: *two bags of rice*.

Pair practice. Make new conversations.

A: *How many boxes of cereal do we need?*
B: *We need two boxes.*

A. **Measure** the ingredients.

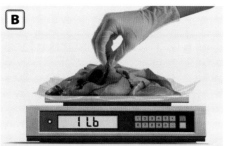

B. **Weigh** the food.

1 cup = 237 milliliters

C. **Convert** the measurements.

Liquid Measures

(1) **1 fl. oz.**

(2) **1 c.**

(3) Frozen Yogurt **1 pt.**

(4) Milk **1 qt.**

(5) **1 gal.**

1. a fluid ounce of milk

2. a cup of oil

3. a pint of frozen yogurt

4. a quart of milk

5. a gallon of water

Dry Measures

(6) SALT **1 tsp.**

(7) SUGAR **1 TBS.**

(8) Brown Sugar **1/4 c.**

(9) **1/2 c.**

(10) FLOUR **1 c.**

6. a teaspoon of salt

7. a tablespoon of sugar

8. a quarter cup of brown sugar

9. a half cup of raisins

10. a cup of flour

Weight

(11)

(12)

11. an ounce of cheese

12. a pound of roast beef

Equivalencies		Volume	Weight
3 tsp. = 1 TBS.	2 c. = 1 pt.	1 fl. oz. = 30 ml	1 oz. = 28.35 grams (g)
2 TBS. = 1 fl. oz.	2 pt. = 1 qt.	1 c. = 237 ml	1 lb. = 453.6 g
8 fl. oz. = 1 c.	4 qt. = 1 gal.	1 pt. = .47 L	2.205 lbs. = 1 kilogram (kg)
		1 qt. = .95 L	1 lb. = 16 oz.
		1 gal. = 3.79 L	

Food Preparation and Safety

Food Safety

A. **clean**

B. **separate**

C. **cook**

D. **chill**

A Clean counters! **20 SECONDS** Wash your hands!

B Use separate cutting boards for vegetables and meat!

C Cook to the right temperature!

D Refrigerate leftovers quickly!

Ways to Serve Meat and Poultry

1. fried chicken

2. barbecued / grilled ribs

3. broiled steak

4. roasted turkey

5. boiled ham

6. stir-fried beef

Ways to Serve Eggs

7. scrambled eggs

8. hard-boiled eggs

9. poached eggs

10. eggs sunny-side up

11. eggs over easy

12. omelet

More vocabulary

bacteria: very small living things that often cause disease
surface: a counter, a table, or the outside part of something
disinfect: to remove bacteria from a surface

Pair practice. Make new conversations.

A: *How do you like your eggs?*
B: *I like them <u>scrambled</u>. And you?*
A: *I like them <u>hard-boiled</u>.*

Cheesy Tofu Vegetable Casserole

A. **Preheat** the oven.

B. **Grease** a baking pan.

C. **Slice** the tofu.

D. **Steam** the broccoli.

E. **Sauté** the mushrooms.

F. **Spoon** sauce on top.

G. **Grate** the cheese.

H. **Bake**.

Easy Chicken Soup

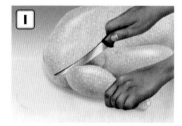

I. **Cut up** the chicken.

J. **Dice** the celery.

K. **Peel** the carrots.

L. **Chop** the onions.

M. **Boil** the chicken.

N. **Add** the vegetables.

O. **Stir**.

P. **Simmer**.

Quick and Easy Cake

Q. **Break** 2 eggs into a microwave-safe bowl.

R. **Mix** the ingredients.

S. **Beat** the mixture.

T. **Microwave** for 5 minutes.

1. can opener
2. grater
3. steamer
4. storage container
5. frying pan
6. pot
7. ladle
8. double boiler

9. wooden spoon
10. casserole dish
11. garlic press
12. carving knife
13. roasting pan
14. roasting rack
15. vegetable peeler
16. paring knife

17. colander
18. kitchen timer
19. spatula
20. eggbeater
21. whisk
22. strainer
23. tongs
24. lid

25. saucepan
26. cake pan
27. cookie sheet
28. pie pan
29. potholders
30. rolling pin
31. mixing bowl

Pair practice. Make new conversations.

A: *Please hand me* <u>the whisk</u>.
B: *Here's* <u>the whisk</u>. *Do you need anything else?*
A: *Yes, pass me* <u>the casserole dish</u>.

Use the new words.
Look at page 77. Name the kitchen utensils you see.

A: *This is* <u>a grater</u>.
B: *This is* <u>a mixing bowl</u>.

1. hamburger	7. nachos	13. ice-cream cone	19. plastic utensils
2. French fries	8. taco	14. milkshake	20. sugar substitute
3. cheeseburger	9. burrito	15. donut	21. ketchup
4. onion rings	10. pizza	16. muffin	22. mustard
5. chicken sandwich	11. soda	17. counterperson	23. mayonnaise
6. hot dog	12. iced tea	18. straw	24. salad bar

Grammar Point: yes/no questions (do)

Do you like hamburgers? Yes, I do.
Do you like nachos? No, I don't.
Practice asking about the food on the page.

Think about it. Discuss.

1. Which fast foods are healthier than others? How do you know?
2. Compare the benefits of a fast food lunch and a lunch from home.

A Coffee Shop Menu

1. bacon
2. sausage
3. hash browns
4. toast
5. English muffin
6. biscuits
7. pancakes
8. waffles
9. hot cereal
10. grilled cheese sandwich
11. pickle
12. club sandwich
13. spinach salad
14. chef's salad
15. house salad / garden salad
16. soup
17. rolls
18. coleslaw
19. potato salad
20. pasta salad
21. fruit salad

Menu

Breakfast Special

Served 6 a.m. to 11 a.m.

Two egg omelet with one side

Lunch

Served 11 a.m. to 2 p.m. • All sandwiches come with soup or salad.

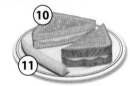

Side salads

18 19 20 21

Dressings

Thousand Island   Ranch   Italian   Blue Cheese

Survey your class. Record the responses.

1. Do you prefer soup or salad?
2. Which do you prefer, tea or coffee?

Report: *Five* of us prefer *tea*. *Most* of us prefer *soup*.

Pair practice. Make new conversations.

A: *What's your favorite side salad?*
B: *I like coleslaw. How about you?*
A: *I like potato salad.*

Dinner

Desserts

Beverages

22. roast chicken

23. mashed potatoes

24. steak

25. baked potato

26. spaghetti

27. meatballs

28. garlic bread

29. grilled fish

30. rice

31. meatloaf

32. steamed vegetables

33. layer cake

34. cheesecake

35. pie

36. mixed berries

37. coffee

38. decaf coffee

39. tea

40. herbal tea

41. cream

42. low-fat milk

Ways to order from a menu

I'd like <u>a grilled cheese sandwich</u>.
I'll have <u>a bowl of tomato soup</u>.
Could I get <u>the chef's salad</u> with <u>ranch dressing</u>?

Role play. Order a dinner from the menu.

A: *Are you ready to order?*
B: *I think so. I'll have <u>the roast chicken</u>.*
A: *Would you also like…?*

A Restaurant

1. dining room
2. hostess
3. high chair
4. booth
5. to-go box
6. patron / diner
7. menu
8. server / waiter

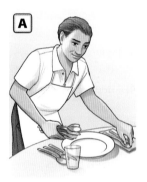

A. **set** the table
B. **seat** the customer
C. **pour** the water

D. **order** from the menu
E. **take** the order
F. **serve** the meal

G. **clear** / **bus** the dishes
H. **carry** the tray
I. **pay** the check

J. **leave** a tip

More vocabulary

eat out: to go to a restaurant to eat
get takeout: to buy food at a restaurant and take it home to eat

Look at the pictures.
Describe what is happening.

A: *She's <u>seating the customer</u>.*
B: *He's <u>taking the order</u>.*

9. server / waitress

10. dessert tray

11. breadbasket

12. busser

13. dish room

14. dishwasher

15. kitchen

16. chef

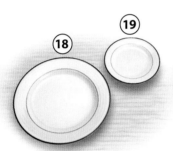

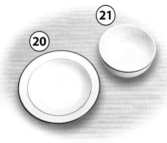

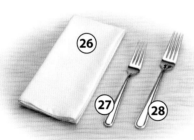

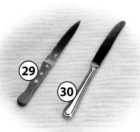

17. place setting

18. dinner plate

19. bread-and-butter plate

20. salad plate

21. soup bowl

22. water glass

23. wine glass

24. cup

25. saucer

26. napkin

27. salad fork

28. dinner fork

29. steak knife

30. knife

31. teaspoon

32. soup spoon

Pair practice. Make new conversations.

A: *Excuse me, this <u>spoon</u> is dirty.*
B: *I'm so sorry. I'll get you a clean <u>spoon</u> right away.*
A: *Thanks.*

Role play. A new busser needs help.

A: *Do the <u>salad forks</u> go on <u>the left</u>?*
B: *Yes. They go <u>next to the dinner forks</u>.*
A: *What about the…?*

The Farmers' Market

1. live music
2. organic
3. lemonade
4. sour
5. samples
6. avocados
7. vendors
8. sweets
9. herbs
A. **count**

What do you see in the picture?

1. How many vendors are at the market today?
2. Which vegetables are organic?
3. What are the children eating?
4. What is the woman counting? Why?

 Read the story.

The Farmers' Market

On Saturdays, the Novaks go to the farmers' market. They like to visit the vendors. Alex Novak always goes to the hot food stand for lunch. His children love to eat the fruit samples. Alex's father usually buys some sweets and lemonade. The lemonade is very sour.

Nina Novak likes to buy organic herbs and vegetables. Today, she is buying avocados. The market worker counts eight avocados. She gives Nina one more for free.

There are other things to do at the market. The Novaks like to listen to the live music. Sometimes they meet friends there. The farmers' market is a great place for families on a Saturday afternoon.

Reread the story.

1. Read the first sentence of the story. How often do the Novaks go to the farmers' market? How do you know?
2. The story says, "The farmers' market is a great place for families." Find examples in the story that support this statement.

What do you think?

3. What's good, bad, or interesting about shopping at a farmers' market?
4. Imagine you are at the farmers' market. What will you buy?

Everyday Clothes

1. shirt

2. jeans

3. dress

4. T-shirt

5. baseball cap

6. socks

7. sneakers

A. **tie**

BEST OF JAZZ CONCERT

TICKETS

BEST OF JAZZ

Listen and point. Take turns.

A: *Point to the dress.*
B: *Point to the T-shirt.*
A: *Point to the baseball cap.*

Dictate to your partner. Take turns.

A: *Write dress.*
B: *Is that spelled d-r-e-s-s?*
A: *Yes, that's right.*

ONE NIGHT ONLY

DOORS OPEN AT 8:00

8. blouse

9. handbag

10. skirt

11. suit

12. slacks / pants

13. shoes

14. sweater

B. **put on**

Ways to compliment clothes

That's a pretty <u>dress</u>!
Those are great <u>shoes</u>!
I really like your <u>baseball cap</u>!

Role play. Compliment a friend.

A: *<u>That's a pretty dress</u>! <u>Green</u> is a great color on you.*
B: *Thanks! I really like your…*

Casual, Work, and Formal Clothes

Casual Clothes

1. cap

2. cardigan sweater

3. pullover sweater

4. sport shirt

5. maternity dress

6. overalls

7. knit top

8. capris

9. sandals

Work Clothes

10. uniform

11. business suit

12. tie

13. briefcase

More vocabulary

in fashion / in style: clothes that are popular now
outfit: clothes that look nice together
three-piece suit: matching jacket, vest, and slacks

Describe the people. Take turns.

A: *She's wearing a maternity dress.*
B: *He's wearing a uniform.*

Formal Clothes

14. sport jacket / sport coat

15. vest

16. bow tie

17. tuxedo

18. evening gown

19. clutch bag

20. cocktail dress

21. high heels

Exercise Wear

22. sweatshirt / hoodie

23. sweatpants

24. tank top

25. shorts

Survey your class. Record the responses.
1. Do you prefer to wear formal or casual clothes?
2. Do you prefer to exercise in shorts or sweatpants?
Report: _25% of the class prefers to…_

Think about it. Discuss.
1. Look at pages 170–173. Which jobs require uniforms?
2. What's good and what's bad about wearing a uniform?
3. Describe a popular style. Do you like it? Why or why not?

Seasonal Clothing

1. hat	5. winter scarf
2. (over)coat	6. gloves
3. headband	7. headwrap
4. leather jacket	8. jacket

9. parka	13. earmuffs
10. mittens	14. down vest
11. ski hat	15. ski mask
12. leggings	16. down jacket

17. umbrella	20. rain boots
18. raincoat	21. trench coat
19. poncho	

22. swimming trunks	25. cover-up
23. straw hat	26. swimsuit / bathing suit
24. windbreaker	27. sunglasses

Grammar Point: should

*It's raining. You **should** take an umbrella.*
*It's snowing. You **should** put on a scarf.*
*It's sunny. You **should** wear a straw hat.*

Pair practice. Make new conversations.

A: *It's <u>snowing</u>. You should put on <u>a scarf</u>.*
B: *Don't worry. I'm wearing my <u>parka</u>.*
A: *Good, and don't forget your <u>mittens</u>!*

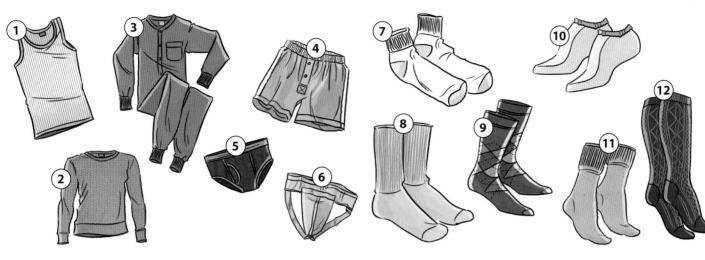

Unisex Underwear

1. undershirt
2. thermal undershirt
3. long underwear

Men's Underwear

4. boxer shorts
5. briefs
6. athletic supporter / jockstrap

Unisex Socks

7. ankle socks
8. crew socks
9. dress socks

Women's Socks

10. low-cut socks
11. anklets
12. knee highs

Women's Underwear

13. (bikini) panties
14. briefs / underpants
15. body shaper / girdle
16. tights
17. footless tights
18. pantyhose
19. bra
20. camisole
21. shapewear slip / slimming slip
22. half slip

Sleepwear

23. pajamas
24. nightgown
25. slippers
26. blanket sleeper
27. nightshirt
28. robe

More vocabulary

lingerie: underwear or sleepwear for women
loungewear: very casual clothing for relaxing around the home

Survey your class. Record the responses.

1. What color socks do you prefer?
2. What type of socks do you prefer?
Report: _Joe prefers white crew socks._

Workplace Clothing

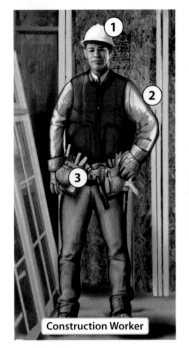

Construction Worker

Road Worker

Automotive Painter

Food Processor

1. hard hat

2. work shirt

3. tool belt

4. high visibility safety vest

5. work pants

6. steel toe boots

7. ventilation mask

8. coveralls

9. bump cap

10. safety glasses

11. apron

Manager

Salesperson

Farmworker

Ranch Hand

12. blazer

13. tie

14. polo shirt

15. name tag

16. bandana

17. work gloves

18. cowboy hat

19. jeans

Use the new words.
Look at pages 170–173. Name the workplace clothing you see.

A: *Look at #37. She's wearing a hard hat.*
B: *Look at #47. He's wearing a lab coat.*

Pair practice. Make sentences.
Dictate them to your classmates.

A. *Farmworkers wear jeans to work.*
B. *A manager often wears a tie to work.*

Security Guard

Emergency Worker

Counterperson

Chef

Line Cook

20. security shirt

21. badge

22. security pants

23. helmet

24. jumpsuit

25. hairnet

26. smock

27. disposable gloves

28. chef's hat

29. chef's jacket

30. waist apron

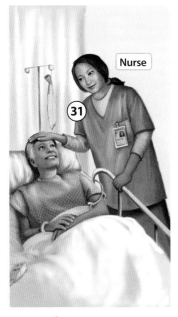

Nurse

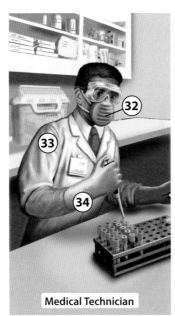

Medical Technician

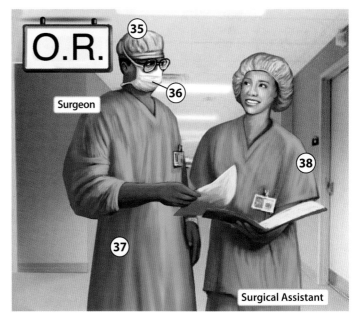

O.R.

Surgeon

Surgical Assistant

31. scrubs

32. face mask

33. lab coat

34. medical gloves

35. surgical scrub cap

36. surgical mask

37. surgical gown

38. surgical scrubs

Identify Anya's problem. Brainstorm solutions.

Anya works at a sandwich counter. Her bus ride to work is an hour. She has to wear a hairnet at work, but today she forgot it at home. What can she do?

Think about it. Discuss.

1. What other jobs require helmets? disposable gloves?
2. Is it better to have a uniform or wear your own clothes at work? Why?

Shoes and Accessories

A. purchase	1. suspenders	3. salesclerk	5. display case
B. wait in line	2. purses / handbags	4. customer	6. belts

13. wallet	17. shoulder bag	21. sole
14. change purse / coin purse	18. backpack	22. heel
15. cell phone case	19. tote bag	23. toe
16. (wrist)watch	20. belt buckle	24. shoelaces

More vocabulary

athletic shoes: tennis shoes, running shoes, etc.
gift / present: something you give to or receive from friends or family for a special occasion

Grammar Point: object pronouns

My **sister** loves jewelry. I'll buy **her** a necklace.
My **dad** likes belts. I'll buy **him** a belt buckle.
My **friends** love scarves. I'll buy **them** scarves.

7. shoe department	9. bracelets	11. hats	C. **try on** shoes
8. jewelry department	10. necklaces	12. scarves	D. **assist** a customer

25. high heels	29. oxfords	33. chain	37. clip-on earrings
26. pumps	30. loafers	34. beads	38. pin
27. flats	31. hiking boots	35. locket	39. string of pearls
28. boots	32. tennis shoes	36. pierced earrings	40. ring

Ways to talk about accessories

I need <u>a hat</u> to wear with <u>this scarf</u>.
I'd like a pair of <u>earrings</u> to match <u>this necklace</u>.
Do you have <u>a belt</u> that would go with my <u>shoes</u>?

Role play. Talk to a salesperson.

A: Do you have <u>boots</u> that would go with <u>this skirt</u>?
B: Let me see. How about <u>these brown ones</u>?
A: Perfect. I also need...

95

Sizes

1. extra small
2. small
3. medium
4. large
5. extra large
6. one-size-fits-all

Styles

7. **crewneck** sweater

8. **V-neck** sweater

9. **turtleneck** sweater

10. **scoop neck** sweater

11. **sleeveless** shirt

12. **short-sleeved** shirt

13. **3/4-sleeved** shirt

14. **long-sleeved** shirt

15. **miniskirt**

16. **short** skirt

17. **mid-length** / **calf-length** skirt

18. **long** skirt

Patterns

19. solid

20. striped

21. polka-dotted

22. plaid

23. print

24. checked

25. floral

26. paisley

Survey your class. Record the responses.

1. What type of sweater do you prefer?
2. What patterns do you prefer?

Report: _Three_ out of _ten_ prefer _____.

Role play. Talk to a salesperson.

A: *Excuse me. I'm looking for this <u>V-neck sweater</u> in <u>large</u>.*
B: *Here's a <u>large</u>. It's on sale for <u>$19.99</u>.*
A: *Wonderful! I'll take it. I'm also looking for…*

Comparing Clothing

27. **heavy** jacket	29. **tight** pants	31. **low** heels	33. **plain** blouse	35. **narrow** tie
28. **light** jacket	30. **loose / baggy** pants	32. **high** heels	34. **fancy** blouse	36. **wide** tie

Clothing Problems

37. It's **too small**.

38. It's **too big**.

39. The zipper is **broken**.

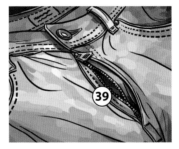

40. A button is **missing**.

41. It's **ripped / torn**.

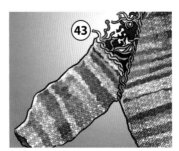

42. It's **stained**.

43. It's **unraveling**.

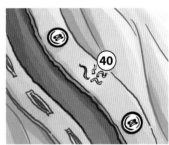

44. It's **too expensive**.

More vocabulary

complaint: a statement that something is not right
customer service: the place customers go with their complaints
refund: money you get back when you return an item to the store

Role play. Return an item to a salesperson.

A: *Welcome to Shopmart. How may I help you?*
B: *This sweater is new, but it's unraveling.*
A: *I'm sorry. Would you like a refund?*

97

Making Clothes

Types of Material

1. cotton

2. linen

3. wool

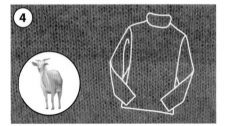

4. cashmere

5. silk

6. leather

A Garment Factory

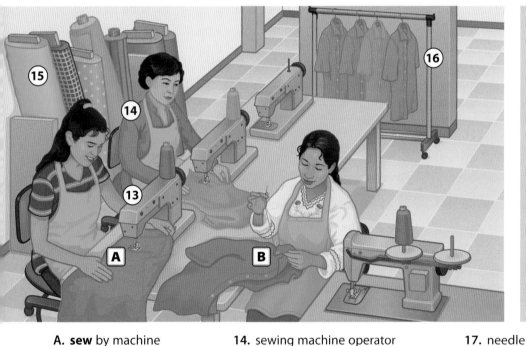

Parts of a Sewing Machine

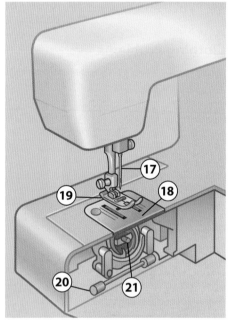

A. **sew** by machine

B. **sew** by hand

13. sewing machine

14. sewing machine operator

15. bolt of fabric

16. rack

17. needle

18. needle plate

19. presser foot

20. feed dog / feed bar

21. bobbin

More vocabulary

fashion designer: a person who draws original clothes
natural materials: cloth made from things that grow in nature
synthetic materials: cloth made by people, such as nylon

Use the new words.
Look at pages 86–87. Name the materials you see.

A: *Look at her pants. They're denim.*
B: *Look at his shoes. They're leather.*

Types of Material

7. denim

8. suede

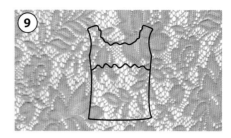

9. lace

10. velvet

11. corduroy

12. nylon

A Fabric Store

22. pattern

23. thread

24. button

25. zipper

26. snap

27. hook and eye

28. buckle

29. hook and loop fastener

30. ribbon

Closures

24. button
25. zipper
26. snap
27. hook and eye
28. buckle
29. hook and loop fastener

Trim

31. appliqué

32. beads

33. sequins

34. fringe

Survey your class. Record the responses.

1. Can you sew?
2. What's your favorite type of material to wear?

Report: *Five* of us can't sew. *Most* of us like to wear *denim*.

Think about it. Discuss.

1. Which jobs require sewing skills?
2. You're going to make a shirt. What do you do first?
3. Which is better, hand sewn or machine sewn? Why?

Making Alterations

An Alterations Shop

1. dressmaker
2. dressmaker's dummy
3. tailor

4. collar
5. waistband
6. sleeve

7. pocket
8. hem
9. cuff

Sewing Supplies

10. needle
11. thread

12. (straight) pin
13. pincushion

14. safety pin
15. thimble

16. pair of scissors
17. tape measure

18. seam ripper

Alterations

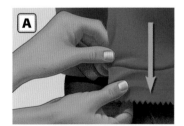

A. **Lengthen** the pants.

B. **Shorten** the pants.

C. **Let out** the pants.

D. **Take in** the pants.

Pair practice. Make new conversations.

A: *Would you hand me the thread?*
B: *OK. What are you going to do?*
A: *I'm going to take in these pants.*

Survey your class. Record the responses.

1. How many pockets do you have?
2. How many pairs of scissors do you have at home?
Report: *Most of us have two ___.*

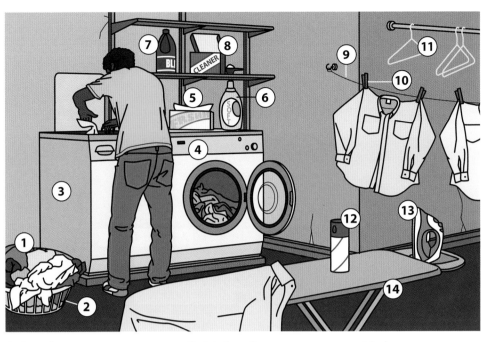

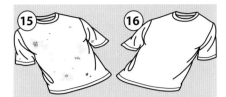

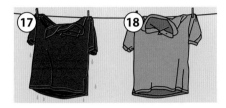

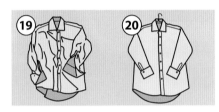

1. laundry
2. laundry basket
3. washer
4. dryer
5. dryer sheets

6. fabric softener
7. bleach
8. laundry detergent
9. clothesline
10. clothespin

11. hanger
12. spray starch
13. iron
14. ironing board
15. **dirty** T-shirt

16. **clean** T-shirt
17. **wet** shirt
18. **dry** shirt
19. **wrinkled** shirt
20. **ironed** shirt

A. **Sort** the laundry.
B. **Add** the detergent.
C. **Load** the washer.
D. **Clean** the lint trap.

 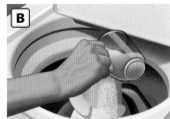  

E. **Unload** the dryer.
F. **Fold** the laundry.
G. **Iron** the clothes.
H. **Hang up** the clothes.

 wash in cold water

 line dry

 no bleach

 dry clean only, do not wash

Pair practice. Make new conversations.

A: *I have to sort the laundry. Can you help?*
B: *Sure. Here's the laundry basket.*
A: *Thanks a lot!*

101

A Garage Sale

1. flyer
2. used clothing
3. sticker
4. folding card table
5. folding chair
6. clock radio
7. VCR
8. CD / cassette player

A. **bargain**
B. **browse**

What do you see in the pictures?

1. What kinds of used clothing do you see?
2. What information is on the flyer?
3. Why are the stickers different colors?
4. How much is the clock radio? the VCR?

 Read the story.

A Garage Sale

Last Sunday, I had a garage sale. At 5:00 a.m., I put up <u>flyers</u> in my neighborhood. Next, I put price <u>stickers</u> on my <u>used clothing</u>, my <u>VCR</u>, my <u>CD / cassette player</u>, and some other old things. At 7:00 a.m., I opened my <u>folding card table</u> and <u>folding chair</u>. Then I waited.

At 7:05 a.m., my first customer arrived. She asked, "How much is the sweatshirt?"

"Two dollars," I said.

She said, "It's stained. I can give you seventy-five cents." We <u>bargained</u> for a minute and she paid $1.00.

All day people came to <u>browse</u>, bargain, and buy. At 7:00 p.m., I had $85.00.

Now I know two things: garage sales are hard work, and nobody wants to buy an old <u>clock radio</u>!

Reread the story.

1. Look at the conversation. Circle the punctuation you see. What do you notice?

What do you think?

2. Do you like to buy things at garage sales? Why or why not?
3. Imagine you want the VCR. How will you bargain for it?

The Body

1. head

2. hair

3. neck

4. chest

5. back

6. nose

7. mouth

8. foot

Listen and point. Take turns.

A: *Point to the chest.*

B: *Point to the neck.*

A: *Point to the mouth.*

Dictate to your partner. Take turns.

A: *Write hair.*

B: *Did you say hair?*

A: *That's right, h-a-i-r.*

9. leg

10. toe

11. eye

12. ear

13. shoulder

14. arm

15. hand

16. finger

Grammar Point: imperatives

Please **touch** your right foot.

Put your hands on your knees.

Don't put your hands on your shoulders.

Pair practice. Take turns giving commands.

A: _Raise_ your _arms_.

B: _Touch_ your _feet_.

A: _Put_ your _hand_ on your _shoulder_.

105

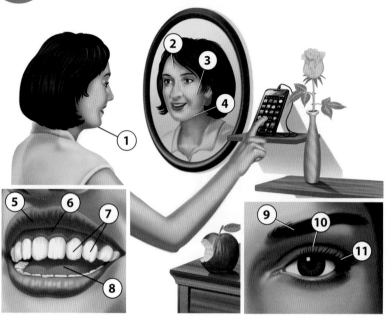

The Face

1. chin
2. forehead
3. cheek
4. jaw

The Mouth

5. lip
6. gums
7. teeth
8. tongue

The Eye

9. eyebrow
10. eyelid
11. eyelashes

The Senses

A. **see**
B. **hear**
C. **smell**
D. **taste**
E. **touch**

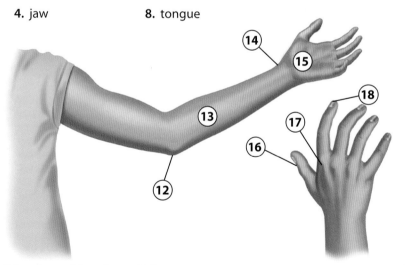

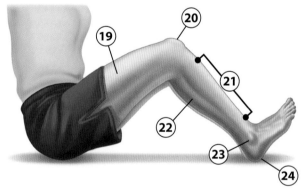

The Arm, Hand, and Fingers

12. elbow
13. forearm
14. wrist
15. palm
16. thumb
17. knuckle
18. fingernail

The Leg and Foot

19. thigh
20. knee
21. shin
22. calf
23. ankle
24. heel

More vocabulary

torso: the part of the body from the shoulders to the pelvis
limbs: arms and legs
toenail: the nail on your toe

Pair practice. Make new conversations.

A: *Is your <u>wrist</u> OK?*
B: *Yes, but now my <u>elbow</u> hurts.*
A: *I'm sorry to hear that.*

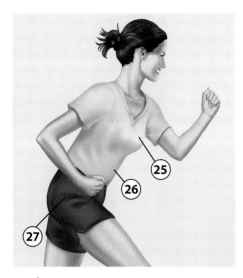

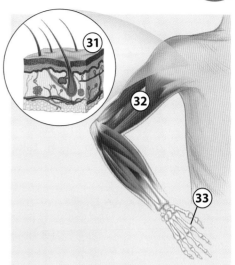

25. breast

26. abdomen

27. hip

28. shoulder blade

29. lower back

30. buttocks

31. skin

32. muscle

33. bone

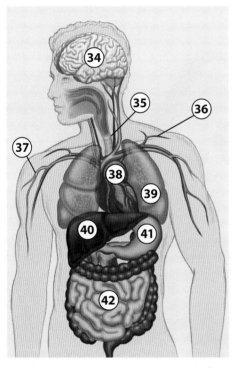

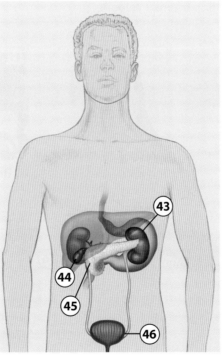

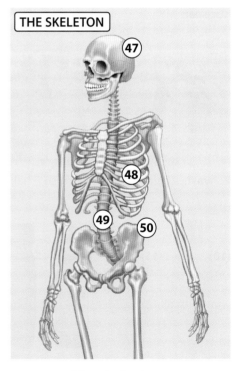

THE SKELETON

34. brain

35. throat

36. artery

37. vein

38. heart

39. lung

40. liver

41. stomach

42. intestines

43. kidney

44. gallbladder

45. pancreas

46. bladder

47. skull

48. rib cage

49. spinal column

50. pelvis

Personal Hygiene

 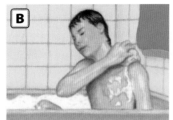  

A. take a shower / **shower**   **B. take** a bath / **bathe**   **C. use** deodorant   **D. put on** sunscreen

1. shower cap

2. shower gel

3. soap

4. bath powder

5. deodorant / antiperspirant

6. perfume / cologne

7. sunscreen

8. sunblock

9. body lotion / moisturizer

E. wash…hair   **F. rinse**…hair   **G. comb**…hair   **H. dry**…hair   **I. brush**…hair

10. shampoo

11. conditioner

12. hairspray

13. comb

14. brush

15. pick

16. hair gel

17. curling iron

18. blow dryer

19. hair clip

20. barrette

21. bobby pins

More vocabulary

hypoallergenic: a product that is better for people with allergies

unscented: a product without perfume or scent

Think about it. Discuss.

1. Which personal hygiene products are most important to use before a job interview? Why?

2. What is the right age to start wearing makeup? Why?

Personal Hygiene

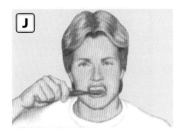

J. brush...teeth

K. floss...teeth

L. gargle

M. shave

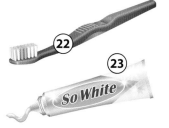

22. toothbrush

23. toothpaste

24. dental floss

25. mouthwash

26. electric shaver

27. razor

28. razor blade

29. shaving cream

30. aftershave

N. cut...nails

O. polish...nails

P. put on / apply

Q. take off / remove

Makeup

31. nail clippers

32. emery board

33. nail polish

34. eyebrow pencil

35. eye shadow

36. eyeliner

37. blush

38. lipstick

39. mascara

40. foundation

41. face powder

42. makeup remover

 1
 2
 3
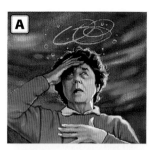 A

 4
 5
 6
 B

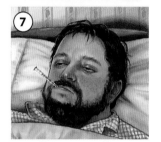 7
 8
 9
 C

1. headache	4. stomachache	7. fever / temperature	A. **feel** dizzy
2. toothache	5. backache	8. chills	B. **feel** nauseous
3. earache	6. sore throat	9. cough	C. **throw up / vomit**

 10
 11
 12
 13

 14
 15
 16
 17

10. insect bite

11. bruise

12. cut

13. sunburn

14. sprained ankle

15. bloody nose

16. swollen finger

17. blister

18. accident report

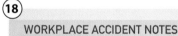

18

WORKPLACE ACCIDENT NOTES

Name: Thiu An
Job Title: Packer
Date of accident: Monday, 9/18/17
Location of accident:
warehouse, aisle 3
Description of accident:
3 boxes fell on me
Was safety equipment used?
☑ yes   ☐ no
Were you injured? yes, sprained wrist
and some bruises

PLEASE FILL OUT A COMPLETE ACCIDENT
FORM AS SOON AS POSSIBLE.

Look at the pictures.
Describe the symptoms and injuries.
A: *He has a backache.*
B: *She has a toothache.*

Think about it. Discuss.
1. What do you recommend for a stomachache?
2. What is the best way to stop a bloody nose?
3. Who should stay home from work with a cold? Why?

Medical Care

In the Waiting Room

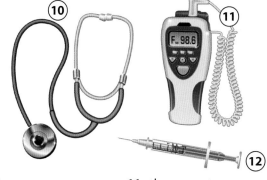

Health Form

Name: *Andre Zolmar*
Date of birth: *July 8, 1983*
Current symptoms: *stomachache*

Health History:

Childhood Diseases:
☑ chicken pox
☑ diphtheria
☑ rubella
☑ measles
☐ mumps
☐ other

Description of symptoms:

HEALTH FIRST
Name: Andre Zolmar
Group Number: 98765
Membership Number: 60756789

1. appointment
2. receptionist
3. health insurance card
4. health history form

In the Examining Room

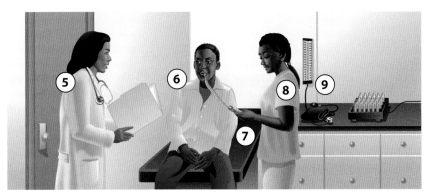

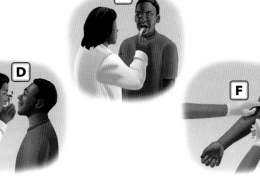

5. doctor
6. patient
7. examination table
8. nurse
9. blood pressure gauge
10. stethoscope
11. thermometer
12. syringe

Medical Procedures

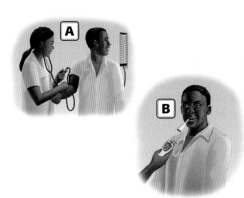

A. **check**…blood pressure

B. **take**…temperature

C. **listen** to…heart

D. **examine**…eyes

E. **examine**…throat

F. **draw**…blood

Grammar Point: future tense with *will* + verb

To describe a future action, use *will* + verb.
The contraction of *will* is *-'ll*.
*She **will draw** your blood.* = *She**'ll draw** your blood.*

Role play. Talk to a medical receptionist.

A: *Will the nurse <u>examine my eyes</u>?*
B: *No, but she'll <u>draw your blood</u>.*
A: *What will the doctor do?*

111

Patient

First name

Last name

Reason for visit

_____ _____ _____

Common Illnesses

1. cold

2. flu

3. ear infection

4. strep throat

Medical History
Childhood and Infectious Diseases

Vaccination date

5. measles   _____

6. chicken pox   _____

7. mumps   _____

8. shingles   _____

9. hepatitis   _____

10. pneumonia   _____

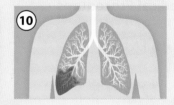

11. allergies

animals   shellfish   peanuts   drugs

I am allergic to:

_____

_____

_____

Survey your class. Record the responses.

1. Are you allergic to cats?
2. Are you allergic to shellfish?

Report: _Five of us are allergic to ____._

Identify Omar's problem. Brainstorm solutions.

Omar filled out only half of the medical history form at the clinic. Many words on the form were new to him, and two questions were very personal. The nurse was upset.

Allergic Reactions

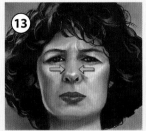

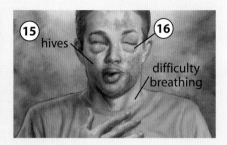

hives

difficulty breathing

12. sneezing   13. nasal congestion   14. rash   15. anaphylaxis   16. swelling

Medical Conditions

	Patient Yes No	Family History		Patient Yes No	Family History
17. cancer	☐ ☐	_____	23. TB / tuberculosis	☐ ☐	_____
18. asthma	☐ ☐	_____	24. high blood pressure / hypertension	☐ ☐	_____
19. dementia	☐ ☐	_____	25. intestinal parasites	☐ ☐	_____
20. arthritis	☐ ☐	_____	26. diabetes	☐ ☐	_____
21. HIV / AIDS	☐ ☐	_____	27. kidney disease	☐ ☐	_____
22. malaria	☐ ☐	_____	28. heart disease	☐ ☐	_____

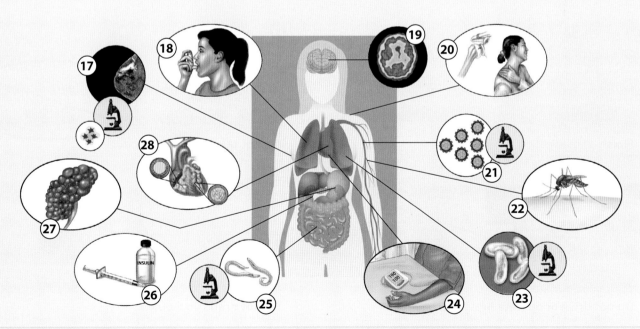

More vocabulary

AIDS (acquired immune deficiency syndrome): a medical condition that results from contracting the HIV virus

Alzheimer's disease: a disease that causes dementia

coronary disease: heart disease

infectious disease: a disease that is spread through air or water

influenza: flu

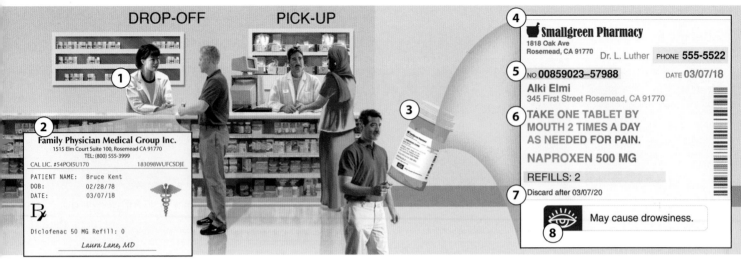

DROP-OFF   PICK-UP

Family Physician Medical Group Inc.
1515 Elm Court Suite 100, Rosemead CA 91770
TEL: (800) 555-3999
CAL LIC. #54POI5U170   183098WUFCSDJE

PATIENT NAME: Bruce Kent
DOB: 02/28/78
DATE: 03/07/18

℞

Diclofenac 50 MG Refill: 0

Laura Lane, MD

Smallgreen Pharmacy
1818 Oak Ave
Rosemead, CA 91770   Dr. L. Luther PHONE **555-5522**

NO **00859023–57988**   DATE **03/07/18**

Alki Elmi
345 First Street Rosemead, CA 91770

**TAKE ONE TABLET BY
MOUTH 2 TIMES A DAY
AS NEEDED FOR PAIN.**

NAPROXEN 500 MG

REFILLS: 2

Discard after 03/07/20

👁 May cause drowsiness.

1. pharmacist
2. prescription
3. prescription medication
4. prescription label
5. prescription number
6. dosage
7. expiration date
8. warning label

Medical Warnings

A

A. **Take** with food or milk.

B 5:00 / 6:00

B. **Take** one hour before eating.

C

JULY

C. **Finish** all medication.

D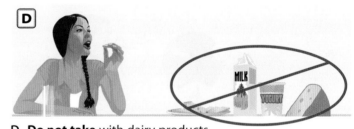

MILK YOGURT

D. **Do not take** with dairy products.

E

E. **Do not drive or operate** heavy machinery.

F

Lite

F. **Do not drink** alcohol.

More vocabulary

prescribe medication: to write a prescription
fill prescriptions: to prepare medications for patients
pick up a prescription: to get prescription medication

Role play. Talk to the pharmacist.

A: *Hi. I need to pick up a prescription for <u>Jones</u>.*
B: *Here's your medication, <u>Mr. Jones</u>. Take these <u>once a day with milk or food</u>.*

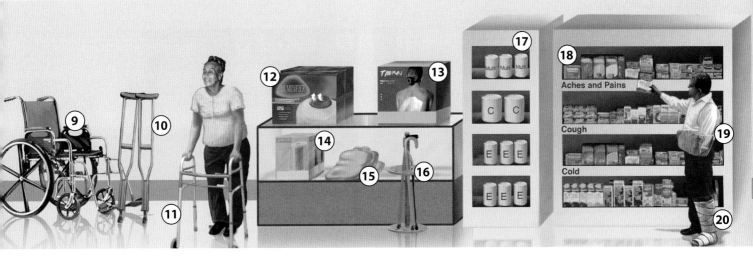

9. wheelchair	13. heating pad	17. vitamins
10. crutches	14. air purifier	18. over-the-counter medication
11. walker	15. hot water bottle	19. sling
12. humidifier	16. cane	20. cast

Types of Medication

21. pill	22. tablet	23. capsule	24. ointment	25. cream

Over-the-Counter Medication

26. pain reliever	28. antacid	30. throat lozenges	32. nasal spray
27. cold tablets	29. cough syrup	31. eye drops	33. inhaler

Ways to talk about medication

Use *take* for pills, tablets, capsules, and cough syrup.
Use *apply* for ointments and creams.
Use *use* for drops, nasal sprays, and inhalers.

Identify Dara's problem. Brainstorm solutions.

Dara's father is 85 and lives alone. She lives nearby.
Her dad has many prescriptions. He often forgets to
take his medication or takes the wrong pills.

Ways to Get Well

A. **Seek** medical attention.

B. **Get** bed rest.

C. **Drink** fluids.

D. **Take** medicine.

Ways to Stay Well

E. **Stay** fit.

F. **Eat** a healthy diet.

G. **Don't smoke**.

H. **Have** regular checkups.

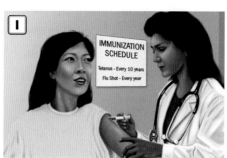

I. **Get** immunized.

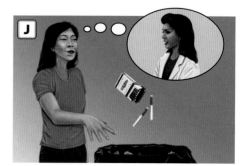

J. **Follow** medical advice.

More vocabulary

injection: medicine in a syringe that is put into the body

immunization / vaccination: an injection that stops serious diseases

Survey your class. Record the responses.

1. How do you stay fit?
2. Which two foods are a part of your healthy diet?

Report: *I surveyed* <u>ten</u> *people who said they* ____.

Types of Health Problems

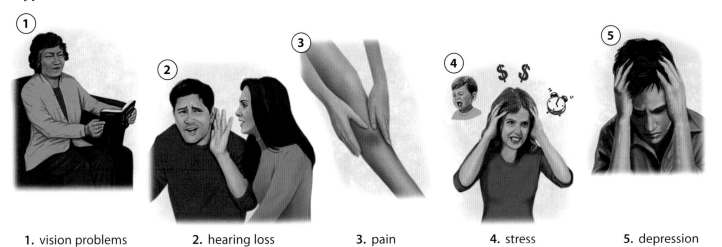

1. vision problems
2. hearing loss
3. pain
4. stress
5. depression

Help with Health Problems

6. optometrist
8. contact lenses
9. audiologist
10. hearing aid

7. glasses

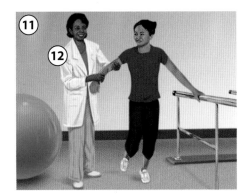

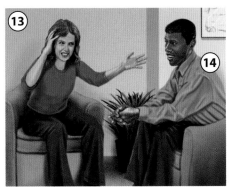

11. physical therapy
13. talk therapy
15. support group

12. physical therapist
14. therapist

Ways to ask about health problems	Pair practice. Make new conversations.
Are you in pain?	**A:** *Do you know a good optometrist?*
Are you having vision problems?	**B:** *Why? Are you having vision problems?*
Are you experiencing depression?	**A:** *Yes, I might need glasses.*

Medical Emergencies

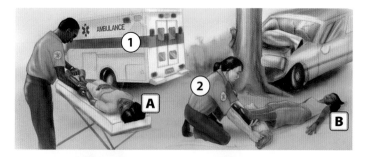

 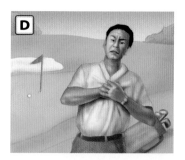

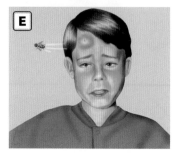   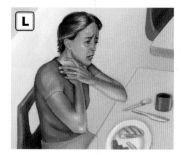

 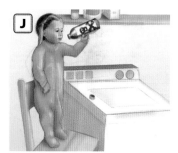 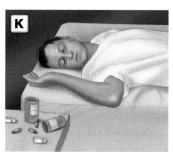

  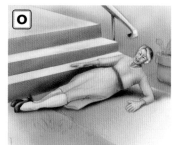 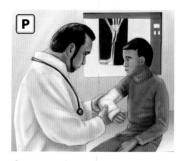

1. ambulance

2. paramedic

A. **be** unconscious

B. **be** in shock

C. **be** injured / **be** hurt

D. **have** a heart attack

E. **have** an allergic reaction

F. **get** an electric shock

G. **get** frostbite

H. **burn** (your)self

I. **drown**

J. **swallow** poison

K. **overdose** on drugs

L. **choke**

M. **bleed**

N. **can't breathe**

O. **fall**

P. **break** a bone

Grammar Point: past tense

For past tense, add **-d** or **-ed**.
burn**ed**, drown**ed**, swallow**ed**,
overdose**d**, chok**ed**

These verbs are different (irregular):

be – was, were	bleed – bled	break – broke
have – had	can't – couldn't	
get – got	fall – fell	

118

First Aid

1. first aid kit

2. first aid manual

3. medical emergency bracelet

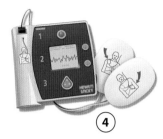

4. AED / automated external defibrillator

Inside the Kit

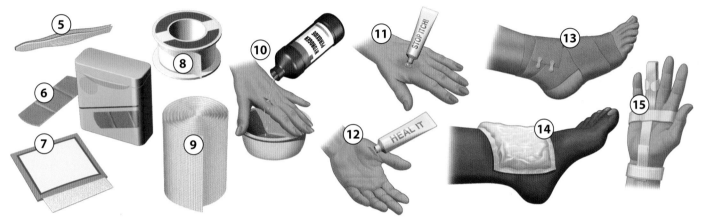

5. tweezers

6. adhesive bandage

7. sterile pad

8. sterile tape

9. gauze

10. hydrogen peroxide

11. antihistamine cream

12. antibacterial ointment

13. elastic bandage

14. ice pack

15. splint

First Aid Procedures

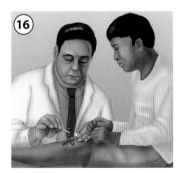

16. stitches

17. rescue breathing

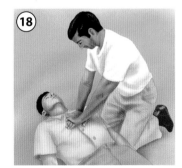

18. CPR (cardiopulmonary resuscitation)

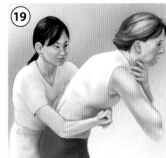

19. Heimlich maneuver

Pair practice. Make new conversations.

A: *What do we need in the first aid kit?*
B: *We need <u>tweezers</u> and <u>gauze</u>.*
A: *I think we need <u>sterile tape</u>, too.*

Internet Research: first aid class

Type "first aid," "class," and your ZIP code in the search bar. Look for a class near you.
Report: *I found a first aid class at ____.*

Dental Care

Dentistry

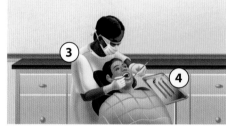

1. dentist
2. dental assistant
3. dental hygienist
4. dental instruments

Orthodontics

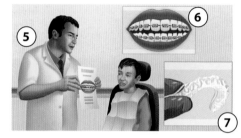

5. orthodontist
6. braces
7. clear aligner

Dental Problems

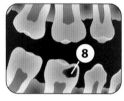
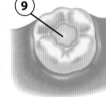

8. cavity / decay
9. filling
10. crown
11. dentures
12. gum disease
13. plaque

An Office Visit

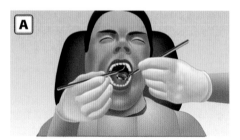

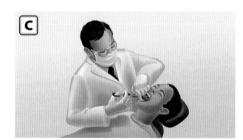

A. **clean** the teeth
B. **take** X-rays
C. **numb** the mouth

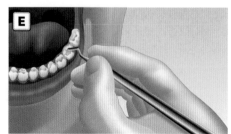

D. **drill** a tooth
E. **fill** a cavity
F. **pull** a tooth

Role play. Talk to a dentist.

A: *I think I have a cavity.*
B: *Let me see. Yes. I will need to drill that tooth.*
A: *Oh! How much will that cost?*

Identify Leo's problem. Brainstorm solutions.

Leo has a bad toothache. His wife says, "Call the dentist." Leo doesn't want to call. He takes pain medication. The toothache doesn't stop.

	BRONZE	SILVER	GOLD
Monthly Premium	$	$$	$$$
Deductible	$5,000	$3,000	$1,500
Co-pay	$35	$30	none
Out-of-pocket Maximum	$10,000	$6,000	$3,000

A

8 That's $35. We'll bill your insurance for the other $115.

B

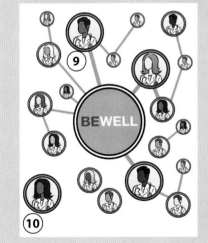

BEWELL HEALTH EXPLANATION OF BENEFITS

Claim submitted: 5/9/18   Provider: **ABC Radiology**

Claim processed: 6/1/18   Patient #5792321

Service Date	Type of Service	Total Billed	Allowable Amount	Co-pay	Amount Paid
5/9/18	X-ray	150.00	150.00	35.00	115.00

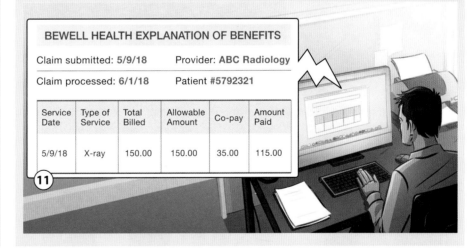

1. carrier
2. insurance plans
3. benefits
4. insurance policy
5. insured / policyholder
6. dependents
7. premium
8. co-pay
9. in-network doctor
10. out-of-network doctor
11. explanation of benefits / EOB
A. **compare** plans
B. **pay** a claim

Medical Specialists

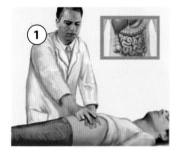

1. internist

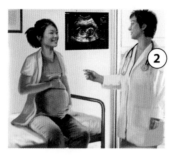

2. obstetrician

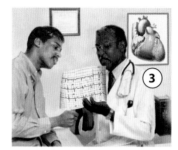

3. cardiologist

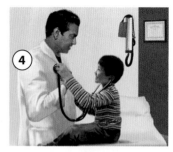

4. pediatrician

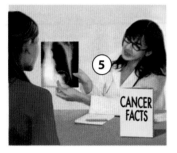

5. oncologist

6. radiologist

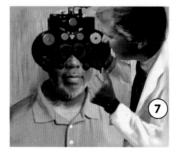

7. ophthalmologist

8. psychiatrist

Nursing Staff

9. surgical nurse

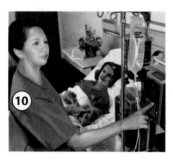

10. registered nurse (RN)

11. licensed practical nurse (LPN)

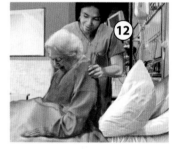

12. certified nursing assistant (CNA)

Hospital Staff

13. administrator

14. admissions clerk

15. dietician

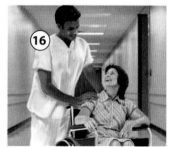

16. orderly

More vocabulary

Gynecologists examine and treat women.
Nurse practitioners can give medical exams.
Nurse midwives deliver babies.

Chiropractors move the spine to improve health.
Orthopedists treat bone and joint problems.
Dermatologists treat skin conditions.
Urologists treat bladder and kidney problems.

A Hospital Room

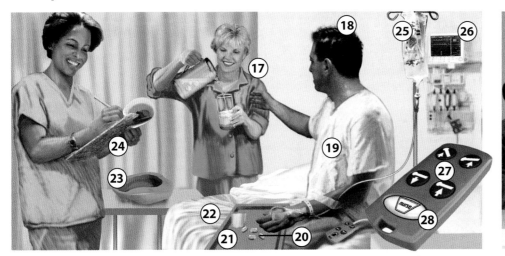

Lab

17. volunteer
18. patient
19. hospital gown
20. medication

21. bed table
22. hospital bed
23. bedpan
24. medical chart

25. IV (intravenous drip)
26. vital signs monitor
27. bed control
28. call button

29. phlebotomist
30. blood work / blood test
31. medical waste disposal

Emergency Room Entrance

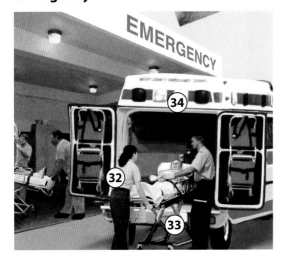

Operating Room

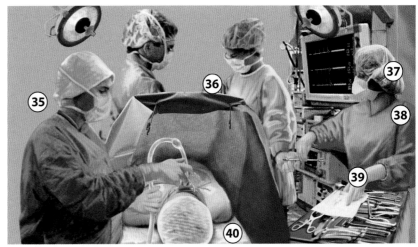

32. emergency medical technician (EMT)
33. stretcher / gurney
34. ambulance

35. anesthesiologist
36. surgeon

37. surgical cap
38. surgical gown

39. surgical gloves
40. operating table

Dictate to your partner. Take turns.

A: *Write this sentence: She's a volunteer.*
B: *She's a what?*
A: *Volunteer. That's v-o-l-u-n-t-e-e-r.*

Role play. Ask about a doctor.

A: *I need to find a good surgeon.*
B: *Dr. Jones is a great surgeon. You should call him.*
A: *I will! Please give me his number.*

A Health Fair

1. low-cost exam
2. acupuncture
3. booth
4. yoga
5. aerobic exercise
6. demonstration
7. sugar-free
8. nutrition label
A. **check**...pulse
B. **give** a lecture

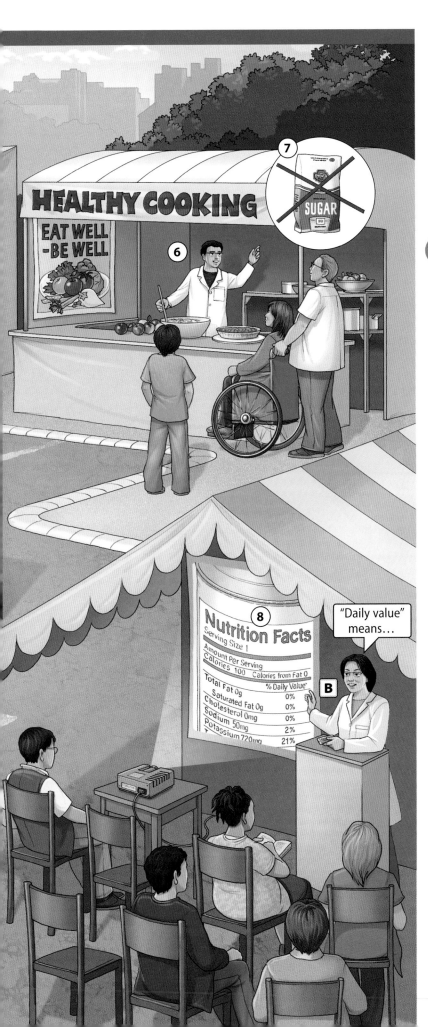

What do you see in the picture?

1. Where is this health fair?
2. What kinds of exams and treatments can you get at this fair?
3. What kinds of lectures and demonstrations can you attend here?
4. How much money should you bring? Why?

Read the article.

A Health Fair

Once a month the Fadool Health Clinic has a health fair. You can get a low-cost medical exam at one booth. The nurses check your blood pressure and check your pulse. At another booth, you can get a free eye exam. And an acupuncture treatment is only $5.00.

You can learn a lot at the fair. This month a doctor is giving a lecture on nutrition labels. There is also a demonstration on sugar-free cooking. You can learn to do aerobic exercise and yoga, too.

Do you want to get healthy and stay healthy? Then come to the Fadool Health Clinic Fair! We want to see you there!

Reread the article.

1. Who wrote this article? How do you know?
2. What information in the picture is *not* in the article?

What do you think?

3. Which booths at this fair look interesting to you? Why?
4. Do you read nutrition labels? Why or why not?

125

Downtown

1. parking garage

2. office building

3. hotel

4. Department of Motor Vehicles

5. bank

6. police station

7. bus station

8. city hall

Listen and point. Take turns.

A: *Point to the bank.*
B: *Point to the hotel.*
A: *Point to the restaurant.*

Dictate to your partner. Take turns.

A: *Write bank.*
B: *Is that spelled b-a-n-k?*
A: *Yes, that's right.*

9. hospital

10. gas station

11. post office

12. fire station

13. courthouse

14. restaurant

15. library

Grammar Point: *in* and *at* with locations

Use *in* when you are inside the building. *I am in (inside) the bank*. Use *at* to describe your general location. *I am at the bank*.

Pair practice. Make new conversations.

A: *I'm in the <u>bank</u>. Where are you?*
B: *I'm at the <u>bank</u>, too, but I'm outside.*
A: *OK. I'll meet you there.*

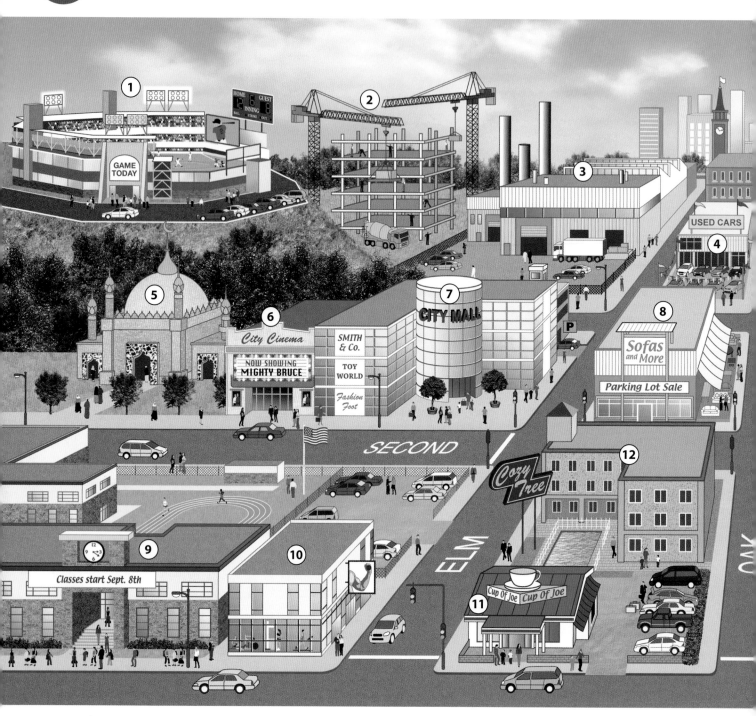

1. stadium

2. construction site

3. factory

4. car dealership

5. mosque

6. movie theater

7. shopping mall

8. furniture store

9. school

10. gym

11. coffee shop

12. motel

Ways to state your destination using *to* and *to the*

Use *to* for schools, churches, and synagogues.
I'm going to <u>school</u>.
Use *to the* for all other locations. *I have to go **to the** <u>bakery</u>.*

Pair practice. Make new conversations.

A: *Where are you going today?*
B: *I'm going to <u>school</u>. How about you?*
A: *I have to go to the <u>bakery</u>.*

13. skyscraper / high-rise

14. church

15. cemetery

16. synagogue

17. community college

18. supermarket

19. bakery

20. home improvement store

21. office supply store

22. garbage truck

23. theater

24. convention center

Ways to give locations

The mall is on Second Street.
The mall is on the corner of Second and Elm.
The mall is next to the movie theater.

Survey your class. Record the responses.

1. Do you have a favorite coffee shop? Which one?
2. Which supermarkets do you go to?
Report: *Nine* out of *ten* students go to ____.

1. laundromat
2. dry cleaners
3. convenience store
4. pharmacy
5. parking space
6. handicapped parking

7. corner
8. traffic light
9. bus
10. fast food restaurant
11. drive-thru window
12. newsstand

13. mailbox
14. pedestrian
15. crosswalk

A. **cross** the street
B. **wait for** the light
C. **jaywalk**

More vocabulary

do errands: to make a short trip from your home to buy or pick up things

neighborhood: the area close to your home

Pair practice. Make new conversations.

A: *I have a lot of errands to do today.*
B: *Me too. First, I'm going to the laundromat.*
A: *I'll see you there after I stop at the copy center.*

16. bus stop	**22.** bike	**28.** cart
17. donut shop	**23.** pay phone	**29.** street vendor
18. copy center	**24.** sidewalk	**30.** childcare center
19. barbershop	**25.** parking meter	**D. ride** a bike
20. used book store	**26.** street sign	**E. park** the car
21. curb	**27.** fire hydrant	**F. walk** a dog

Internet Research: finding business listings

Type "pharmacy" and your city in the search bar. Count the pharmacy listings you see.

Report: *I found 25 pharmacies in Chicago.*

Think about it. Discuss.

1. How many different jobs are there at this intersection?
2. Which of these businesses would you like to own? Why?

1. music store
2. jewelry store
3. nail salon
4. bookstore
5. toy store
6. pet store
7. card store
8. florist
9. optician
10. shoe store
11. play area
12. guest services

More vocabulary

beauty shop: hair salon

gift shop: a store that sells T-shirts, mugs, and other small gifts

men's store: men's clothing store

Pair practice. Make new conversations.

A: *Where is the florist?*

B: *It's on the first floor, next to the optician.*

13. department store

14. travel agency

15. food court

16. ice cream shop

17. candy store

18. hair salon

19. maternity store

20. electronics store

21. elevator

22. kiosk

23. escalator

24. directory

Ways to talk about plans

Let's go to the <u>card store</u>.
I have to go to the <u>card store</u>.
I want to go to the <u>card store</u>.

Role play. Talk to a friend at the mall.

A: *Let's go to the <u>card store</u>. I need to buy <u>a card</u> for Maggie's birthday.*
B: *OK, but can we go to the <u>shoe store</u> next?*

The Bank

1. teller

2. customer

3. deposit

4. deposit slip

5. security guard

6. vault

7. safety deposit box

8. valuables

Bank Accounts

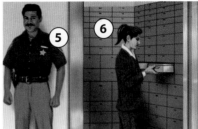

9. account manager

10. joint account

11. opening deposit

12. ATM card

13. checkbook

14. check

15. checking account number

16. savings account number

A. **Cash** a check.

B. **Make** a deposit.

17. bank statement

18. balance

The ATM (Automated Teller Machine)

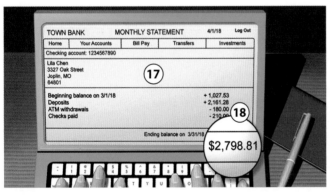

C. **Insert** your ATM card.

D. **Enter** your PIN.*

E. **Withdraw** cash.

F. **Remove** your card.

*PIN = personal identification number

A. get a library card

B. look for a book

C. check out a book

D. return a book

E. pay a late fine

1. library clerk	4. periodicals	7. headline	10. self-checkout
2. circulation desk	5. magazine	8. atlas	11. online catalog
3. library patron	6. newspaper	9. reference librarian	12. picture book

13. biography	15. author	17. audiobook	19. DVD
14. title	16. novel	18. e-book	

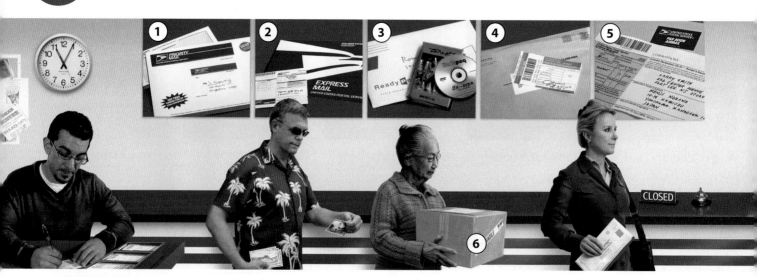

1. Priority Mail®
2. Express Mail®
3. Media Mail®
4. Certified Mail™
5. airmail
6. ground post / parcel post

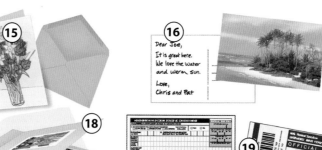

13. letter
14. envelope
15. greeting card
16. postcard
17. package
18. book of stamps
19. postal forms
20. letter carrier

Sonya Enriquez
258 Quentin Avenue
Los Angeles, CA 90068-1416

Cindy Lin
807 Glenn Drive
Charlotte, NC 28201

21. return address
22. mailing address
23. stamp
24. postmark

Ways to talk about sending mail

This letter has to <u>get there tomorrow</u>. (Express Mail®)
This letter has to <u>arrive in two days</u>. (Priority Mail®)
This letter can go in <u>regular mail</u>. (First Class)

Pair practice. Make new conversations.

A: Hi. <u>This letter has to get there tomorrow</u>.
B: You can send it by <u>Express Mail</u>®.
A: OK. I need <u>a book of stamps</u>, too.

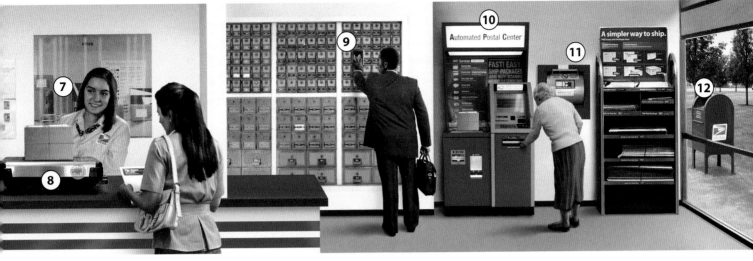

7. postal clerk

8. scale

9. post office box (PO box)

10. automated postal center (APC)

11. post office lobby drop

12. mailbox

Sending a Card

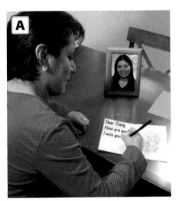

A. **Write** a note in a card.

B. **Address** the envelope.

C. **Put on** a stamp.

D. **Mail** the card.

E. **Deliver** the card.

F. **Receive** the card.

G. **Read** the card.

H. **Write** back.

More vocabulary

junk mail: mail you don't want
overnight / next-day mail: Express Mail®
postage: the cost to send mail

Survey your class. Record the responses.

1. Do you send greeting cards by mail or online?
2. Do you pay bills by mail or online?
Report: _25% of us send cards by mail_.

137

1. DMV handbook

2. testing area

3. DMV clerk

4. photo

5. fingerprint

6. vision exam

7. window

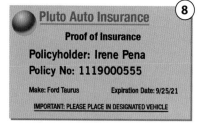

8. proof of insurance

9. driver's license

10. expiration date

11. driver's license number

12. license plate

13. registration sticker / tag

More vocabulary

expire: A license is no good, or **expires**, after the expiration date.

renew a license: to apply to keep a license before it expires

vanity plate: a more expensive, personal license plate

Internet Research: DMV locations

Type "DMV" and your ZIP code in the search bar. How many DMVs are there?

Report: *I found _____ DMV office(s) near me.*

Getting Your First License

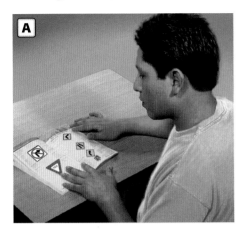

A. **Study** the handbook.

B. **Take** a driver education course.*

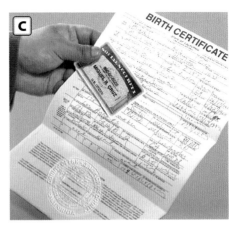

C. **Show** your identification.

D. **Pay** the application fee.

E. **Take** a written test.

F. **Get** a learner's permit.

G. **Take** a driver's training course.*

H. **Pass** a driving test.

I. **Get** your license.

*Note: This is not required for drivers 18 and older.

Ways to request more information	**Role play. Talk to a DMV clerk.**
What do I do next?	**A:** *I want to apply for <u>a driver's license</u>.*
What's the next step?	**B:** *Did you <u>study the handbook</u>?*
Where do I go from here?	**A:** *Yes, I did. <u>What do I do next</u>?*

Government and Military Service

Federal Government

Legislative Branch

1. U.S. Capitol
2. Congress
3. House of Representatives
4. congressperson
5. Senate
6. senator

Executive Branch

7. White House
8. president
9. vice president
10. Cabinet

Judicial Branch

11. Supreme Court
12. justices
13. chief justice

State Government

14. governor
15. lieutenant governor
16. state capital

17. Legislature
18. assemblyperson
19. state senator

City Government

20. mayor
21. city council
22. councilperson

The U.S. Military

23. Pentagon

24. Secretary of Defense

25. general

26. admiral

27. officer

Military Service

A. **be** a recruit

B. **be** on active duty

C. **be** on reserve

D. **be** a veteran

Branches of the Military

28. Army

29. soldier

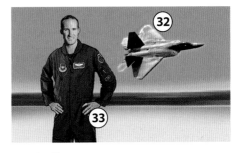

30. Navy

31. seaman / sailor

32. Air Force

33. airman

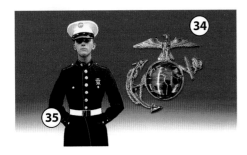

34. Marines

35. marine

36. Coast Guard

37. coast guardsman

38. National Guard*

39. national guardsman

*Each state has an Army National Guard. The national guardsmen are reservists.

Civic Engagement

Responsibilities

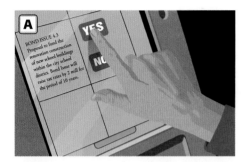

A. vote

B. pay taxes

C. obey the law

D. register with Selective Service*

E. serve on a jury

F. be informed

Citizenship Requirements

G. be 18 or older

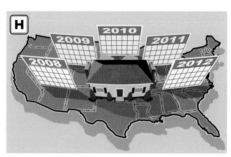

H. live in the U.S. for five years

I. take a citizenship test

Rights

1. peaceful assembly

2. free speech

3. freedom of religion

4. freedom of the press

5. a fair trial

*****Note:** All males 18 to 26 who live in the U.S. are required to register with Selective Service.

An Election

J. run for office   **6.** candidate

K. campaign   **7.** rally

L. debate   **8.** opponent

9. ballot   **10.** voting booth / polling booth

M. get elected   **11.** election results

N. serve   **12.** elected official

More vocabulary

political party: a group of people with the same political goals

term: the period of time an elected official serves

Think about it. Discuss.

1. Should everyone have to vote? Why or why not?
2. Are candidate debates important? Why or why not?
3. Would you prefer to run for city council or mayor? Why?

143

A. *You have the right to remain silent…*

A. arrest a suspect

1. police officer
2. handcuffs

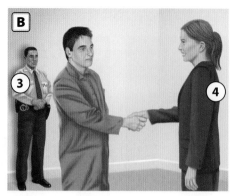

B. hire a lawyer / **hire** an attorney

3. guard
4. defense attorney

C. *Bail is set at $20,000.*

C. appear in court

5. defendant
6. judge

D. stand trial

7. courtroom
8. jury
9. evidence
10. prosecuting attorney
11. witness
12. court reporter
13. bailiff

E. *Guilty.*

E. convict the defendant

14. verdict*

F. *7 years*

F. sentence the defendant

G. go to jail / **go** to prison

15. convict / prisoner

H. be released

*Note: There are two possible verdicts, "guilty" and "not guilty."

Look at the pictures.
Describe what happened.

A: *The police officer arrested a suspect*.
B: *He put handcuffs on him*.

Think about it. Discuss.

1. Would you want to serve on a jury? Why or why not?
2. Look at the crimes on page 145. What sentence would you give for each crime? Why?

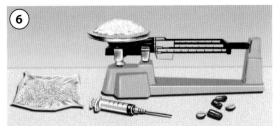

1. vandalism

2. burglary

3. assault

4. gang violence

5. drunk driving

6. illegal drugs

7. arson

8. shoplifting

9. identity theft

10. victim

11. mugging

12. murder

13. gun

More vocabulary

commit a crime: to do something illegal
criminal: someone who does something illegal
steal: to take money or things from someone illegally

Identify the tenants' problem. Brainstorm solutions.

The apartment tenants at 65 Elm Street are upset.
There were three burglaries on their block last month.
This month there were five burglaries and a mugging!

Public Safety

A. **Walk** with a friend.

B. **Stay** on well-lit streets.

C. **Conceal** your PIN number.

D. **Protect** your purse or wallet.

E. **Lock** your doors.

F. Don't **open** your door to strangers.

G. Don't **drink** and **drive**.

H. **Shop** on secure websites.

I. **Be** aware of your surroundings.

J. **Report** suspicious packages.

K. **Report** crimes to the police.

L. **Join** a Neighborhood Watch.

More vocabulary

sober: not drunk
designated drivers: sober drivers who drive drunk people home safely

Survey your class. Record the responses.

1. Do you always lock your doors?
2. Do you belong to a Neighborhood Watch?

Report: _75% of us always lock our doors._

Online Dangers for Children

1. cyberbullying
2. online predators
3. inappropriate material

Ways to Protect Children

A. **Turn on** parental controls.
B. **Monitor** children's Internet use.
C. **Block** inappropriate sites.

Internet Crime

4. phishing
5. hacking

Safety Solutions

D. **Create** secure passwords.
E. **Update** security software.
F. **Use** encrypted / secure sites.
G. **Delete** suspicious emails.

Emergencies and Natural Disasters

1. lost child

2. car accident

3. airplane crash

4. explosion

5. earthquake

6. mudslide

7. forest fire

8. fire

9. firefighter

10. fire truck

Ways to report an emergency

First, give your name. *My name is <u>Tim Johnson</u>.*
Then, state the emergency and give the address.
There was <u>a car accident</u> at <u>219 Elm Street</u>.

Role play. Call 911.

A: *911 emergency operator.*
B: *My name is <u>Lisa Diaz</u>. There is <u>a fire</u> at <u>323 Oak Street</u>.
Please hurry!*

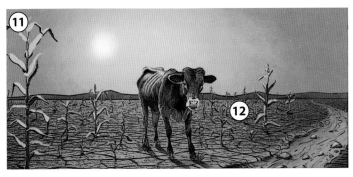

11. drought

12. famine

13. blizzard

14. hurricane

15. tornado

16. volcanic eruption

17. tidal wave / tsunami

18. avalanche

19. flood

20. search and rescue team

Survey your class. Record the responses.

1. Which natural disaster worries you the most?
2. Which natural disaster worries you the least?

Report: _Five_ of us are _most_ worried about _earthquakes_.

Think about it. Discuss.

1. What organizations can help you in an emergency?
2. What are some ways to prepare for natural disasters?
3. Where would you go in an emergency?

149

Before an Emergency

A. **Plan** for an emergency.

1. meeting place

2. out-of-state contact

3. escape route

4. gas shut-off valve

5. evacuation route

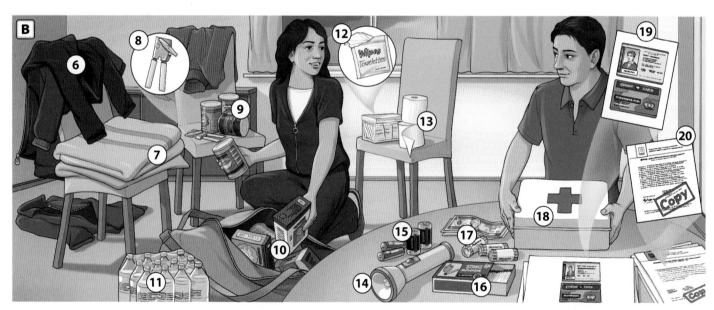

B. **Make** a disaster kit.

6. warm clothes

7. blankets

8. can opener

9. canned food

10. packaged food

11. bottled water

12. moist towelettes

13. toilet paper

14. flashlight

15. batteries

16. matches

17. cash and coins

18. first aid kit

19. copies of ID and credit cards

20. copies of important papers

Pair practice. Make new conversations.

A: *What do we need for our disaster kit?*
B: *We need blankets and matches.*
A: *I think we also need batteries.*

Survey your class. Record the responses.

1. Do you have a disaster kit?
2. Do you have an out-of-state contact?
Report: *Ten of us have a disaster kit.*

During an Emergency

C. Watch the weather.

D. Pay attention to warnings.

E. Remain calm.

F. Follow directions.

G. Help people with disabilities.

H. Seek shelter.

I. Stay away from windows.

J. Take cover.

K. Evacuate the area.

After an Emergency

L. Call out-of-state contacts.

M. Clean up debris.

N. Inspect utilities.

Ways to say you're OK

I'm fine.
We're OK here.
Everything's under control.

Ways to say you need help

We need help.
Someone is hurt.
I'm injured. Please get help.

Role play. Prepare for an emergency.

A: *They just issued a hurricane warning.*
B: *OK. We need to stay calm and follow directions.*
A: *What do we need to do first?*

151

Community Cleanup

1. graffiti
2. litter
3. streetlight
4. hardware store
5. petition
A. **give** a speech
B. **applaud**
C. **change**

What do you see in the pictures?

1. What were the problems on Main Street?

2. What was the petition for?

3. Why did the city council applaud?

4. How did the volunteers change the street?

📄 **Read the story.**

Community Cleanup

Marta Lopez has a donut shop on Main Street. One day she looked at her street and was very upset. She saw <u>graffiti</u> on her donut shop and the other stores. <u>Litter</u> was everywhere. All the <u>streetlights</u> were broken. Marta wanted to fix the lights and clean up the street.

Marta started a <u>petition</u> about the streetlights. Five hundred people signed it. Then she <u>gave a speech</u> to the city council. The council members voted to repair the streetlights. Everyone <u>applauded</u>. Marta was happy, but her work wasn't finished.

Next, Marta asked for volunteers to clean up Main Street. The <u>hardware store</u> manager gave the volunteers free paint. Marta gave them free donuts and coffee. The volunteers painted and cleaned. They <u>changed</u> Main Street. Now Main Street is beautiful and Marta is proud.

Reread the story.

1. Find "repair" in paragraph 2. Find another word for "repair" in the story.

What do you think?

2. What are the benefits of being a volunteer?

3. What do you think Marta said in her speech? How do you know?

Basic Transportation

1. car

2. passenger

3. taxi

4. motorcycle

5. street

6. truck

7. train

8. (air)plane

Listen and point. Take turns.

A: *Point to the motorcycle.*
B: *Point to the truck.*
A: *Point to the train.*

Dictate to your partner. Take turns.

A: *Write motorcycle.*
B: *Could you repeat that for me?*
A: *I said motorcycle.*

9. helicopter

10. airport

11. subway station

12. subway

13. bus stop

14. bus

15. bicycle

Ways to talk about using transportation
Use *take* for buses, trains, subways, taxis, planes, and helicopters. Use *drive* for cars and trucks. Use *ride* for bicycles and motorcycles.

Pair practice. Make new conversations.
A: *How do you get to school?*
B: *I take the bus. How about you?*
A: *I ride a bicycle to school.*

Public Transportation

A Bus Stop

BUS 10 Northbound

Main	Elm	Oak
6:00	6:10	6:13
6:30	6:40	6:43
7:00	7:10	7:13
7:30	7:40	7:43

TRANSFER →

Valid for $2\frac{1}{2}$ hours

1. bus route
2. fare
3. rider
4. schedule
5. transfer

A Subway Station

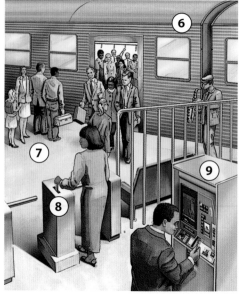

MetroCard

6. subway car
7. platform
8. turnstile
9. vending machine
10. token
11. fare card

A Train Station

AMTRAK

LIZ   LK98S
KOENIG   3/12/2017

TRIP
CHICAGO, IL   5:15 PM
ST. LOUIS, MO 10:45 PM

RAIL FARE 70.00
PAYMENT STATUS PAID
RAIL PLANS G0517B
ISSUE CHICAGO UNION STATION
TICKET 1 OF 1

Fresno

Los Angeles

Fresno

Los Angeles

12. ticket window
13. conductor
14. track
15. ticket
16. one-way trip
17. round trip

Airport Transportation

18. TAXIS

19. J&J Hotel

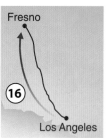

18. taxi stand
19. shuttle
20. town car
21. taxi driver
22. taxi license
23. meter

More vocabulary

hail a taxi: to raise your hand to get a taxi
miss the bus: to get to the bus stop after the bus leaves

Internet Research: taxi fares

Type "taxi fare finder" and your city in the search bar.
Enter a starting address and an ending address.
Report: *The fare from my house to school is $10.00.*

A. go under the bridge **B. go over** the bridge **C. walk up** the steps **D. walk down** the steps

E. get into the taxi **F. get out of** the taxi **G. run across** the street **H. run around** the corner

I. get on the highway **J. get off** the highway **K. drive through** the tunnel

Grammar Point: *into, out of, on, off*

Use *get into* for taxis and cars.
Use *get on* for buses, trains, planes, and highways.

Use *get out of* for taxis and cars.
Use *get off* for buses, trains, planes, and highways.

1. stop

2. do not enter / wrong way   **3.** one way

4. speed limit

5. U-turn OK

6. no outlet / dead end

7. right turn only

8. no left turn

9. yield

10. merge

11. no parking

12. handicapped parking

13. pedestrian crossing   **15.** school crossing   **17.** U.S. route / highway marker

14. railroad crossing   **16.** roadwork   **18.** hospital

Pair practice. Make new conversations.

A: *Watch out! The sign says <u>no left turn</u>.*
B: *Sorry, I was looking at the <u>stop</u> sign.*
A: *That's OK. Just be careful!*

Survey your class. Record the responses.

1. Which traffic signs are different in your native country?
2. Which traffic signs are similar in your native country?
Report: *The U.S. and <u>Mexico</u> have similar <u>stop</u> signs.*

Directions

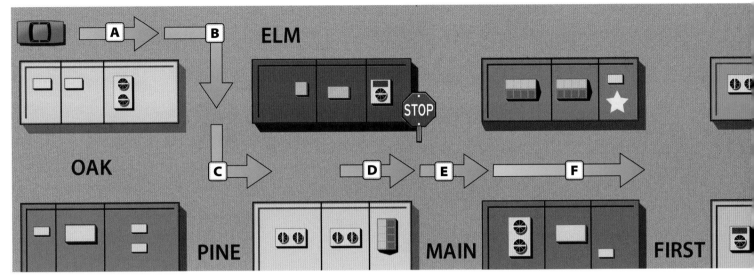

A. Go straight on Elm Street.

B. Turn right on Pine Street.

C. Turn left on Oak Street.

D. Stop at the corner.

E. Go past Main Street.

F. Go one block to First Street.

Maps

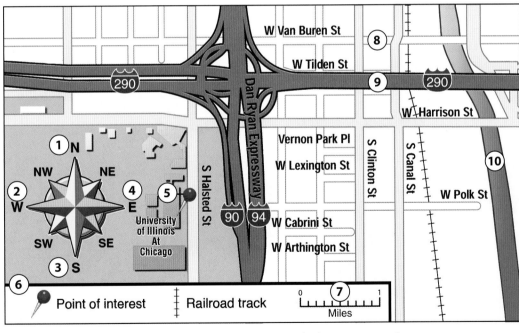

1. north
2. west
3. south
4. east
5. symbol
6. key
7. scale
8. street
9. highway
10. river
11. GPS (global positioning system)
12. Internet map

Role play. Ask for directions.

A: *I'm lost. I need to get to Elm and Pine.*
B: *Go straight on Oak and make a right on Pine.*
A: *Thanks so much.*

Think about it. Discuss.

1. What are the pros and cons of using a GPS?
2. Which types of jobs require map-reading skills?

1. hybrid

2. electric vehicle / EV

3. EV charging station

4. sports car

5. convertible

6. hatchback

7. SUV (sport utility vehicle)

8. minivan

9. camper

10. RV (recreational vehicle)

11. limousine / limo

12. pickup truck

13. cargo van

14. tow truck

15. tractor-trailer / semi

16. cab

17. trailer

18. moving van

19. dump truck

20. tank truck

21. school bus

More vocabulary

sedan: a 4-door car

coupe: a 2-door car

make and model: the car manufacturer and style: *Ford Fiesta*

Pair practice. Make new conversations.

A: *I have a new car!*

B: *Did you get a hybrid?*

A: *Yes, but I really wanted a sports car.*

Buying a Used Car

A. **Look at** car ads.

B. **Ask** the seller about the car.

C. **Take** the car to a mechanic.

D. **Negotiate** a price.

E. **Get** the title from the seller.

F. **Register** the car.

Taking Care of Your Car

G. **Fill** the tank with gas.

H. **Check** the oil.

I. **Put in** coolant.

J. **Go** for a smog and safety check.*

K. **Replace** the windshield wipers.

L. **Fill** the tires with air.

*smog check = emissions test

Ways to request service

Please check the oil.
Could you fill the tank?
Put in coolant, please.

Think about it. Discuss.

1. What's good and bad about a used car?
2. Do you like to negotiate car prices? Why or why not?
3. Do you know any good mechanics? Why are they good?

At the Dealer

1. windshield	5. tire
2. windshield wipers	6. turn signal
3. side-view mirror	7. headlight
4. hood	8. bumper

At the Mechanic

9. hubcap / wheel cover	13. taillight
10. gas tank	14. brake light
11. trunk	15. tailpipe
12. license plate	16. muffler

Under the Hood

17. fuel injection system	19. radiator
18. engine	20. battery

Inside the Trunk

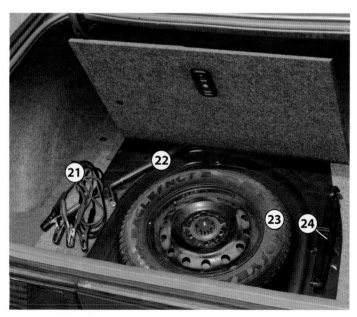

21. jumper cables	23. spare tire
22. lug wrench	24. jack

The Dashboard and Instrument Panel

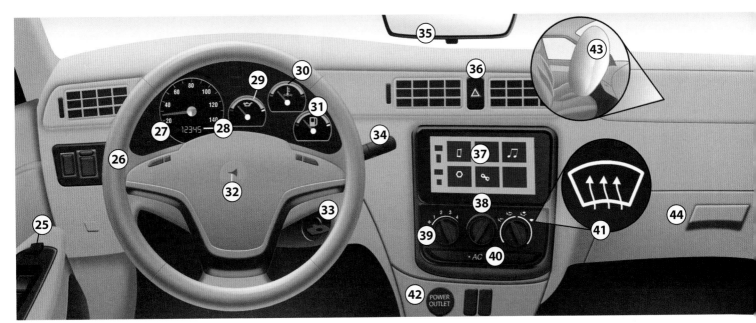

25. door lock

26. steering wheel

27. speedometer

28. odometer

29. oil gauge

30. temperature gauge

31. gas gauge

32. horn

33. ignition

34. turn signal

35. rearview mirror

36. hazard lights

37. touch screen / audio display

38. temperature control dial

39. fan speed

40. air conditioning / AC button

41. defroster

42. power outlet

43. airbag

44. glove compartment

An Automatic Transmission

A Manual Transmission

Inside the Car

45. brake pedal

46. gas pedal / accelerator

47. gearshift

48. handbrake

49. clutch

50. stick shift

51. front seat

52. seat belt

53. child safety seat

54. back seat

An Airport

In the Airline Terminal

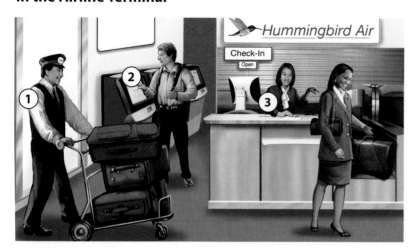

1. skycap
2. check-in kiosk
3. ticket agent
4. screening area

At the Security Checkpoint

5. TSA* agent / security screener
6. bin

Taking a Flight

A. **Check in** electronically.

B. **Check** your bags.

C. **Show** your boarding pass and ID.

D. **Go through** security.

E. **Board** the plane.

F. **Find** your seat.

G. **Stow** your carry-on bag.

H. **Fasten** your seat belt.

I. **Put** your cell phone in airplane mode.

J. **Take off**. / **Leave**.

K. **Land**. / **Arrive**.

L. **Claim** your baggage.

* Transportation Security Administration

At the Gate

On the Airplane

At Customs

7. arrival and departure monitors

8. gate

9. boarding area

10. cockpit

11. pilot

12. flight attendant

13. overhead compartment

14. emergency exit

15. passenger

16. declaration form

17. customs officer

18. luggage / bag

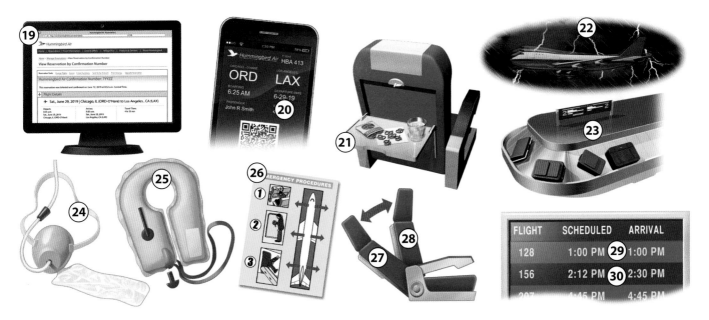

19. e-ticket

20. mobile boarding pass

21. tray table

22. turbulence

23. baggage carousel

24. oxygen mask

25. life vest

26. emergency card

27. reclined seat

28. upright seat

29. on time

30. delayed

More vocabulary

departure time: the time the plane takes off
arrival time: the time the plane lands
nonstop flight: a trip with no stops

Pair practice. Make new conversations.

A: *Excuse me. Where do I* <u>check in</u>?
B: *At the* <u>check-in kiosk</u>.
A: *Thanks.*

A Road Trip

Seattle, WA

YELLOWSTONE NATIONAL PARK

1. ranger

2. wildlife

3. stars

4. scenery

5. automobile club card

6. destination

A. **pack**

B. **be** lost

C. **have** a flat tire

D. **get** a ticket

E. **run out** of gas

F. **break down**

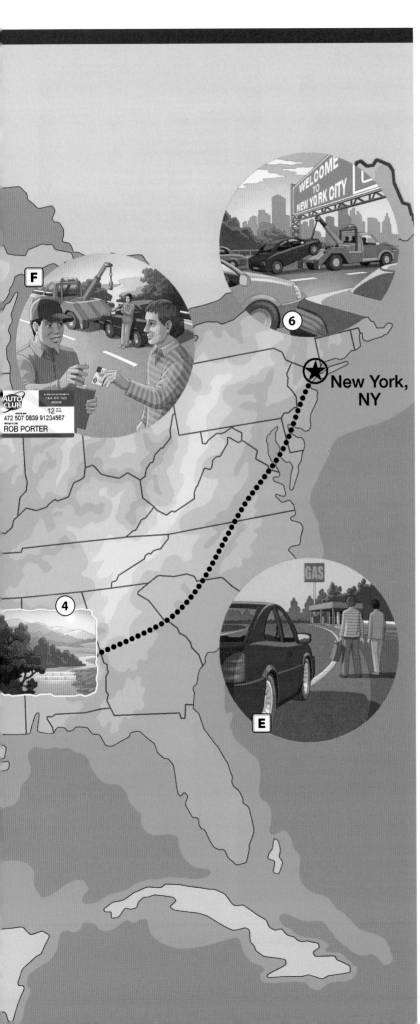

What do you see in the pictures?

1. Where are the young men from? What's their destination?

2. Do they have a good trip? How do you know?

Read the story.

A Road Trip

On July 7, Joe and Rob <u>pack</u> their bags and start their road trip to New York City.

Their first stop is Yellowstone National Park. They listen to a <u>ranger</u> talk about the <u>wildlife</u> in the park. That night they go to bed under a sky full of <u>stars</u>, but Rob can't sleep. He's nervous about the wildlife.

The next day, their GPS breaks. "We're not going in the right direction!" Rob says. "<u>We're lost</u>!"

"No problem," says Joe. "We can take the southern route. We'll see some beautiful <u>scenery</u>."

But there are *a lot* of problems. They <u>have a flat tire</u> in west Texas and <u>get a</u> speeding <u>ticket</u> in east Texas. In South Carolina, they <u>run out of gas</u>. Then, five miles from New York City, their car <u>breaks down</u>. "Now, *this* is a problem," Joe says.

"No, it isn't," says Rob. He calls the number on his <u>automobile club card</u>. Help arrives in 20 minutes.

After 5,000 miles of problems, Joe and Rob finally reach their <u>destination</u>—by tow truck!

Reread the story.

1. Find the phrase "Help arrives." What does that phrase mean?

What do you think?

2. What is good, bad, or interesting about taking a road trip?

3. Imagine you are planning a road trip. Where will you go?

167

Job Search

A. **set** a goal

B. **write** a resume

C. **contact** references

D. **research** local companies

E. **talk** to friends / **network**

F. **go** to an employment agency

G. **look** for help wanted signs

H. **check** employment websites

Listen and point. Take turns.

A: *Point to a resume.*

B: *Point to a help wanted sign.*

A: *Point to an application.*

Dictate to your partner. Take turns.

A: *Write contact.*

B: *Is it spelled c-o-n-t-a-c-t?*

A: *Yes, that's right, contact.*

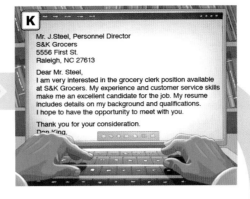

Can you come in for an interview at 9:00?

Tell me about your experience.

I worked in a market for two years.

Take these to aisle 9.

OK!

Mr. King, the job is yours.

I. **apply** for a job

J. **complete** an application

K. **write** a cover letter

L. **submit** an application

M. **set up** an interview

N. **go on** an interview

O. **get** a job / **be** hired

P. **start** a new job

Ways to talk about the job search

It's important to <u>set a goal</u>.
You have to <u>write a resume</u>.
It's a good idea to <u>network</u>.

Role play. Talk about a job search.

A: *I'm looking for a job. What should I do?*
B: *Well, it's important to <u>set a goal</u>.*
A: *Yes, and I have to <u>write a resume</u>.*

1. accountant

2. actor

3. administrative assistant

4. appliance repairperson

5. architect

6. artist

7. assembler

8. auto mechanic

9. babysitter

10. baker

11. business owner

12. businessperson

13. butcher

14. carpenter

15. cashier

16. childcare worker

Ways to ask about someone's job

What's <u>her</u> job?
What does <u>he</u> do?
What does <u>he</u> do for a living?

Pair practice. Make new conversations.

A: *What <u>does she</u> do for a living?*
B: *<u>She's an accountant</u>. What <u>do they</u> do?*
A: *<u>They're actors</u>.*

17. commercial fisher

18. computer software engineer

19. computer technician

We have that shirt in red.

20. customer service representative

21. delivery person

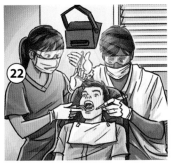

22. dental assistant

23. dock worker

24. electronics repairperson

25. engineer

26. firefighter

27. florist

28. gardener

29. garment worker

30. graphic designer

31. hairdresser / hairstylist

32. home healthcare aide

Ways to talk about jobs and occupations

*Sue's <u>a garment worker</u>. She works **in** a factory.*
*Tom's <u>an engineer</u>. He works **for** a large company.*
Luis is <u>a gardener</u>. He's self-employed.

Role play. Talk about a friend's new job.

A: *Does your friend like <u>his</u> new job?*
B: *Yes, <u>he</u> does. He's <u>a graphic designer</u>.*
A: *Who does <u>he</u> work for?*

171

33. homemaker

34. housekeeper

35. interpreter / translator

36. lawyer

37. machine operator

38. manicurist

39. medical records technician

40. messenger / courier

41. model

42. mover

43. musician

44. nurse

45. occupational therapist

46. (house) painter

47. physician assistant

48. police officer

Grammar Point: past tense of be

*I **was** a machine operator for five years.*
*She **was** a model from 2010 to 2012.*
*Before they **were** movers, they **were** painters.*

Pair practice. Make new conversations.

A: *What was your first job?*
B: *I was <u>a musician</u>. How about you?*
A: *I was <u>a messenger for a small company</u>.*

49. postal worker

50. printer

51. receptionist

52. reporter

53. retail clerk

54. sanitation worker

55. security guard

56. server

57. social worker

58. soldier

59. stock clerk

60. telemarketer

61. truck driver

62. veterinarian

63. welder

64. writer / author

Survey your class. Record the responses.

1. What is one job you don't want to have?
2. Which jobs do you want to have?

Report: *Tom wants to be a(n) ____, but not a(n) ____.*

Think about it. Discuss.

Q: What kind of person makes a good <u>interpreter</u>? Why?
A: To be a(n) ____, you need to be able to ____ and have ____, because…

Planning and Goal Setting

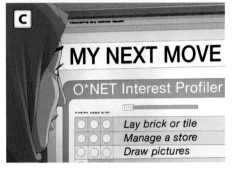

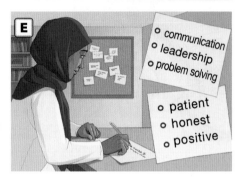

A. **visit** a career planning center

B. **explore** career options

C. **take** an interest inventory

D. **identify** your technical skills

E. **list** your soft skills

F. **consult** with a career counselor

G. **set** a long-term goal

H. **set** a short-term goal

I. **attend** a job fair

J. **speak** with a recruiter

Career Path

1. **1**
2. **2**
3. **3**
4. **4**

1. basic education

2. entry-level job

3. training

4. new job

5 VALLEY COMMUNITY COLLEGE

6 Nurse, can you help me?

7 WHAT'S NEW IN TEXTILES

8 DRESSMART

5. college degree

6. career advancement

7. continuing education / professional development

8. promotion

Types of Training

9
10
11

9. career and technical training / vocational training

10. apprenticeship

11. internship

12. on-the-job training

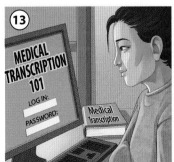

12 Enter the number here.

13 MEDICAL TRANSCRIPTION 101 — LOG IN: PASSWORD: — Medical Transcription

14 The Future of Textiles

13. online course

14. workshop

Job Skills

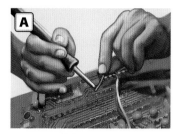

A. **assemble** components

B. **assist** medical patients

C. **cook**

D. **do** manual labor

E. **drive** a truck

F. **fly** a plane

G. **make** furniture

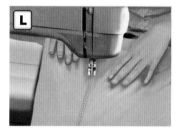

H. **operate** heavy machinery

I. **program** computers

J. **repair** appliances

K. **sell** cars

L. **sew** clothes

M. **solve** math problems

N. **speak** another language

O. **supervise** people

P. **take care of** children

Q. **teach**

R. **type**

S. **use** a cash register

T. **wait on** customers

Grammar Point: *can, can't*

I am a chef. I **can** cook.

I'm not a pilot. I **can't** fly a plane.

I **can't** speak French, but I **can** speak Spanish.

Role play. Talk to a job counselor.

A: *Let's talk about your skills. Can you <u>type</u>?*

B: *<u>No, I can't, but</u> I can <u>use a cash register</u>.*

A: *That's good. What else can you do?*

Office Skills

A. **type** a letter

B. **enter** data

C. **transcribe** notes

D. **make** copies

E. **collate** papers

F. **staple**

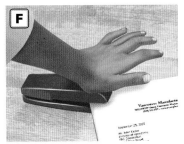

G. **fax** a document

H. **scan** a document

I. **print** a document

J. **schedule** a meeting

K. **take** notes

L. **organize** materials

Telephone Skills

M. **greet** the caller

N. **put** the caller on hold

O. **transfer** the call

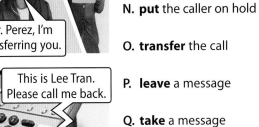

P. **leave** a message

Q. **take** a message

R. **check** messages

Soft Skills

Leadership Skills

A. **solve** problems

B. **think** critically

C. **make** decisions

D. **manage** time

Interpersonal Skills

E. **communicate** clearly

F. **cooperate** with teammates

G. **clarify** instructions

H. **respond** well to feedback

Personal Qualities

1. patient

2. positive

3. willing to learn

4. honest

Ways to talk about your skills
I **can** <u>solve problems</u>. I <u>communicate clearly</u>.
Ways to talk about your qualities
I **am** <u>patient</u> and <u>honest</u>.

Talk about your skills and abilities.
A: *Tell me about your <u>leadership skills</u>.*
B: *I <u>can solve problems</u>. How about you?*
A: *I <u>can think critically</u>.*

 **A**

 **B**

 **C**

A. **Prepare** for the interview.

B. **Dress** appropriately.

C. **Be** neat.

 **D**

 **E**

 **F**

D. **Bring** your resume and ID.

E. **Don't be** late.

F. **Be** on time.

 **G**

 **H**

Hello, I'm Elias Ortiz.

Hello, Mr. Ortiz. I'm Mrs. Perez.

I

G. **Turn off** your cell phone.

H. **Greet** the interviewer.

I. **Shake** hands.

 **J**

 **K**

Computer skills are important.

I have those skills.

 **L**

I worked with computers on my last job.

J. **Make** eye contact.

K. **Listen** carefully.

L. **Talk** about your experience.

 **M**

Do you offer training?

 **N**

Thank you for your time.

 **O**

Dear Mrs. Perez, Thank you for the opportunity to meet with you.

M. **Ask** questions.

N. **Thank** the interviewer.

O. **Write** a thank-you note.

More vocabulary

benefits: health insurance, vacation pay, or other things the employer can offer an employee

inquire about benefits: to ask about benefits

Identify Dan's problem. Brainstorm solutions.

Dan has an interview tomorrow. Making eye contact with strangers is hard for him. He doesn't like to ask questions. What can he do?

First Day on the Job

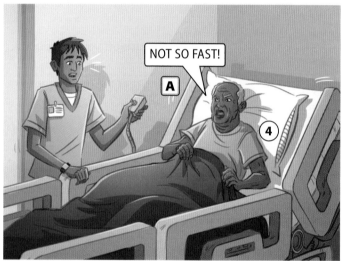

NOT SO FAST!

A

He doesn't know anything!

B

I was an actor.

I was an engineer.

D

1. facility	3. team player	5. co-worker
2. staff	4. resident	6. shift

A. **yell**	C. **direct**
B. **complain**	D. **distribute**

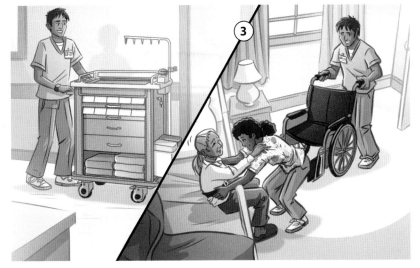

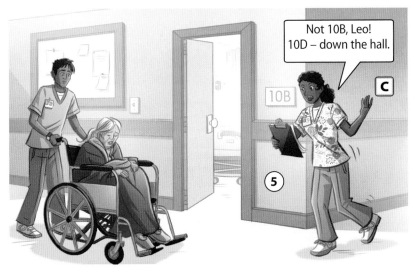

Not 10B, Leo!
10D – down the hall.

10B

C

5

How did it go, Leo?

I learned a lot!

	FROM	TO	CNA STAFF
1ST	7:00AM	3:30PM	MARY, LIZ, LEO
2ND	3:00PM	11:30PM	BEN, SARA, TOM
3RD	11:00PM	7:30AM	MEI, KARA, JOSH

6

What do you see in the pictures?

1. What time does Leo arrive at the nursing home?

2. What other types of workers are on the staff?

3. Is Leo a team player? How do you know?

4. How long was Leo's shift on his first day?

Read the story.

First Day on the Job

Leo Reyes arrives at the Lakeview nursing home <u>facility</u> at 7 a.m. It's his first day as a CNA. The nurse, Ms. Castro, introduces him to the <u>staff</u>. He meets Lakeview's receptionist, cook, social worker, physical therapists, and the other CNAs. Then it's time for work.

Leo has a positive attitude. He is a <u>team player</u>. He also makes mistakes.

One elderly <u>resident</u> <u>yells</u> at Leo. Another <u>complains</u> about him. Leo goes to the wrong room, but a <u>co-worker</u> <u>directs</u> him to the right one.

The afternoon is better. Leo listens to the residents talk about their careers. He drives the van to the mall. He helps another CNA <u>distribute</u> the afternoon snacks.

At the end of his <u>shift</u>, Ms. Castro asks Leo about his day. He tells her, "I worked hard, made mistakes, and learned a lot!" Ms. Castro smiles and says, "Sounds like a good first day!"

Reread the story.

1. Highlight the word "distribute" in paragraph 4. What other words can you use here?

2. Underline two examples of negative feedback in the story.

What do you think?

3. Should Leo respond to the residents' feedback? Why or why not?

181

The Workplace

1. entrance
2. customer
3. office
4. employer / boss
5. receptionist
6. safety regulations

IRINA'S COMPUTER SERVICE

OSHA
HAZARDS
SPILLS
CALL 911
SAFETY FIRST

COMPUTER NEWS

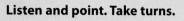
Irina Sarkov Owner

Listen and point. Take turns.

A: *Point to the front entrance.*
B: *Point to the receptionist.*
A: *Point to the time clock.*

Dictate to your partner. Take turns.

A: *Can you spell employer?*
B: *I'm not sure. Is it e-m-p-l-o-y-e-r?*
A: *Yes, that's right.*

7. time clock

8. supervisor

9. employee

10. payroll clerk

11. pay stub

12. wages

13. deductions

14. paycheck

Ways to talk about wages

*I **earn** $800 a week.*
*He **makes** $10 an hour.*
*I'm **paid** $2,000 a month.*

Role play. Talk to an employer.

A: *Is everything correct on your paycheck?*
B: *No, it isn't. I make $619 a week, not $519.*
A: *Let's talk to the payroll clerk. Where is she?*

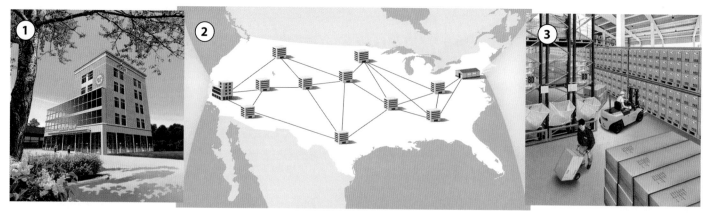

1. corporate offices / headquarters

2. branch locations

3. warehouse

4. human resources

5. research and development

6. marketing

Sales are up!

7. sales

8. logistics

9. accounting

10. IT / information technology

11. customer service

12. building maintenance

13. security

Use the new words.

Look at pages 170–173. Find jobs for each department.

A: *Accountants* work in *accounting*.

B: *Security guards* work in *security*.

Survey your class. Record the responses.

Which department(s) would you like to work in?

Report: *Ten* of us would like to work in *logistics*.

*Nobody wants to work in *security*.

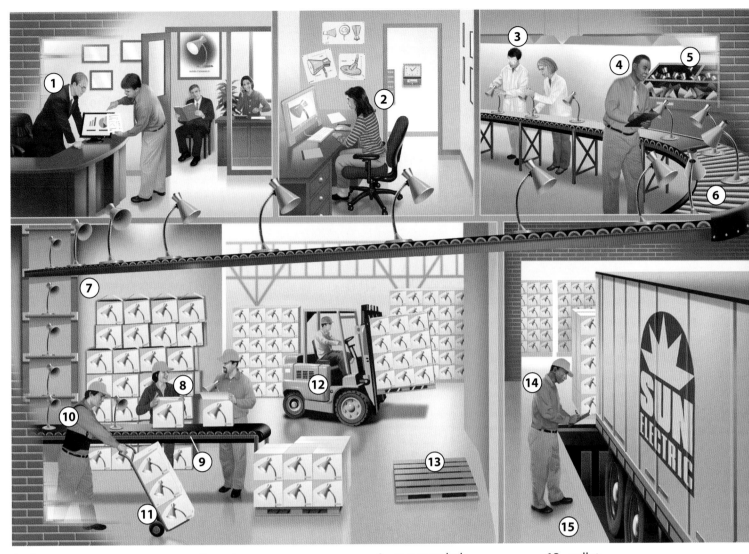

1. factory owner
2. designer
3. factory worker
4. line supervisor

5. parts
6. assembly line
7. warehouse
8. packer

9. conveyer belt
10. order puller
11. hand truck
12. forklift

13. pallet
14. shipping clerk
15. loading dock

A. design

B. manufacture

C. assemble

D. ship

Landscaping and Gardening

1. gardening crew

2. leaf blower

3. wheelbarrow

4. gardening crew leader

5. landscape designer

6. lawn mower

7. shovel

8. rake

9. pruning shears

10. trowel

11. hedge clippers

12. weed whacker / weed eater

A. **mow** the lawn

B. **trim** the hedges

C. **rake** the leaves

D. **fertilize** / **feed** the plants

E. **plant** a tree

F. **water** the plants

G. **weed** the flower beds

H. **install** a sprinkler system

Use the new words.
Look at page 53. Name what you can do in the yard.

A: *I can mow the lawn.*

B: *I can weed the flower bed.*

Identify Inez's problem. Brainstorm solutions.

Inez works on a gardening crew. She wants to learn to install sprinklers. The crew leader has no time to teach her. What can she do?

186

Crops

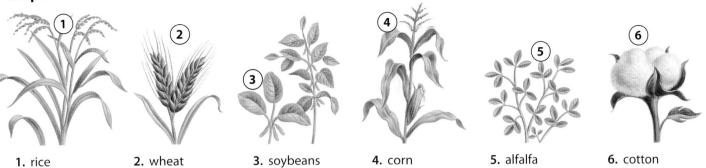

1. rice **2.** wheat **3.** soybeans **4.** corn **5.** alfalfa **6.** cotton

7. field

8. farmworker

9. tractor

10. orchard

11. barn

12. farm equipment

13. farmer / grower

14. vegetable garden

15. livestock

16. vineyard

17. corral

18. hay

19. fence

20. hired hand

21. cattle

22. rancher

A. plant

B. harvest

C. milk

D. feed

1. supply cabinet	5. executive	9. desk	13. PBX
2. clerk	6. presentation	10. file clerk	14. receptionist
3. janitor	7. cubicle	11. file cabinet	15. reception area
4. conference room	8. office manager	12. computer technician	16. waiting area

---

Ways to greet a receptionist

Good <u>morning</u>. I'm here for a <u>job interview</u>.
Hello. I have a <u>9 a.m.</u> appointment with <u>Mr. Lee</u>.
Hi. I'm here to see <u>Mr. Lee</u>. <u>He's</u> expecting me.

Role play. Talk to a receptionist.

A: *Hello. How can I help you?*
B: *<u>I'm here for a job interview with Mr. Lee</u>.*
A: *OK. What is your name?*

Office Equipment

17. computer

18. inkjet printer

19. laser printer

20. scanner

21. fax machine

22. paper cutter

23. photocopier

24. paper shredder

25. calculator

26. electric pencil sharpener

27. postal scale

Office Supplies

28. stapler

29. staples

30. clear tape

31. paper clip

32. packing tape

33. glue

34. rubber band

35. pushpin

36. correction fluid

37. correction tape

38. legal pad

39. sticky notes

40. mailer

41. mailing label

42. letterhead / stationery

43. envelope

44. rotary card file

45. ink cartridge

46. ink pad

47. stamp

48. appointment book

49. organizer

50. file folder

Information Technology (IT)

1. mainframe computer   **3.** data   **4.** cybersecurity   **6.** tablet

2. computer operations
    specialist   **5.** virus alert

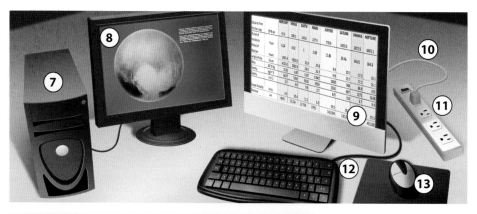

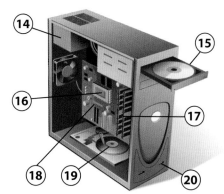

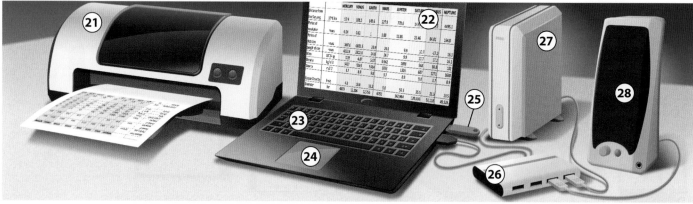

7. tower

8. monitor

9. desktop computer

10. power cord

11. surge protector

12. cable

13. mouse

14. power supply unit

15. DVD and CD-ROM drive

16. microprocessor / CPU

17. RAM (random access
      memory)

18. motherboard

19. hard drive

20. USB port

21. printer

22. laptop computer

23. keyboard

24. track pad

25. flash drive / thumb drive

26. hub

27. external hard drive

28. speaker

Software / Applications

29. word processing program

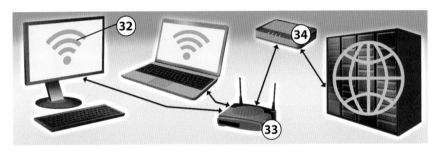

30. spreadsheet program

31. presentation program

Internet Connectivity

32. Wi-Fi connection **34.** modem

33. router

Web Conferencing

35. headset **37.** webcam

36. mic / microphone

A. The computer **won't start**.

B. The screen **froze**.

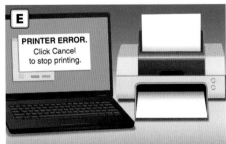

C. I **can't install** the update.

D. I **can't log on**.

E. It **won't print**.

F. I **can't stream** video.

1. doorman

2. revolving door

3. parking attendant

4. concierge

5. gift shop

6. bell captain

7. bellhop

8. luggage cart

9. elevator

10. guest

11. desk clerk

12. front desk

13. guest room

14. double bed

15. king-size bed

16. suite

17. room service

18. hallway

19. housekeeping cart

20. housekeeper

21. pool service

22. pool

23. maintenance

24. gym

25. meeting room

26. ballroom

A Restaurant Kitchen

1. short-order cook

2. dishwasher

3. walk-in freezer

4. food preparation worker

5. storeroom

6. sous-chef

7. head chef / executive chef

Restaurant Dining

8. server

9. diner

10. buffet

11. maitre d'

12. headwaiter

13. bus person

14. banquet room

15. runner

16. caterer

More vocabulary

line cook: short-order cook

wait staff: servers, headwaiters, and runners

Think about it. Discuss.

1. What is the hardest job in a hotel or restaurant? Explain.
   (*Being a _____ is hard because these workers have to _____.*)
2. Pick two jobs on these pages. Compare them.

Tools and Building Supplies

HAND TOOLS

HARDWARE

POWER TOOLS

1. hammer
2. mallet
3. ax

4. handsaw
5. hacksaw
6. C-clamp

7. pliers
8. electric drill
9. circular saw

10. jigsaw
11. power sander
12. router

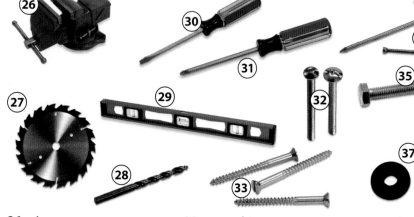

26. vise
27. blade
28. drill bit
29. level

30. screwdriver
31. Phillips screwdriver
32. machine screw
33. wood screw

34. nail
35. bolt
36. nut
37. washer

38. toggle bolt
39. hook
40. eye hook
41. chain

Use the new words.
Look at pages 62–63. Name the tools you see.

A: *There's a hammer.*

B: *There's a pipe wrench.*

Survey your class. Record the responses.

1. Are you good with tools?
2. Which tools do you have at home?

Report: *75% of us are… Most of us have…*

ELECTRICAL   PLUMBING   LUMBER   PAINT

13. wire	**16.** yardstick	**19.** 2 x 4 (two by four)	**22.** paintbrush
14. extension cord	**17.** pipe	**20.** particle board	**23.** paint roller
15. bungee cord	**18.** fittings	**21.** spray gun	**24.** wood stain

25. paint

42. wire stripper	**46.** outlet cover	**50.** plunger	**54.** drop cloth
43. electrical tape	**47.** pipe wrench	**51.** paint pan	**55.** chisel
44. work light	**48.** adjustable wrench	**52.** scraper	**56.** sandpaper
45. tape measure	**49.** duct tape	**53.** masking tape	**57.** plane

Role play. Find an item in a building supply store.

A: *Where can I find <u>particle board</u>?*
B: *It's <u>on the back wall</u>, in the <u>lumber</u> section.*
A: *Great. And where <u>are the nails</u>?*

Identify Jean's problem. Brainstorm solutions.

Jean borrowed Jody's drill last month. Now she can't find it. She doesn't know what to do!

195

1. construction worker
2. ladder
3. I beam / girder

4. scaffolding
5. cherry picker
6. bulldozer

7. crane
8. backhoe
9. jackhammer / pneumatic drill

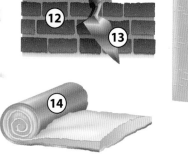

10. concrete
11. tile
12. bricks

13. trowel
14. insulation
15. stucco

16. windowpane
17. wood / lumber
18. plywood

19. drywall
20. shingles
21. pickax

22. shovel
23. sledgehammer

A. paint

B. lay bricks

C. install tile

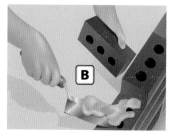

D. hammer

Safety Hazards and Hazardous Materials

1. careless worker

2. careful worker

3. poisonous fumes

4. broken equipment

5. frayed cord

6. slippery floor

7. radioactive materials

8. flammable liquids

Safety Equipment

9. hard hat

10. safety glasses

11. safety goggles

12. safety visor

13. respirator

14. particle mask

15. earplugs

16. earmuffs

17. work gloves

18. back support belt

19. knee pads

20. safety boots

21. fire extinguisher

22. two-way radio

1. dangerous
2. clinic
3. budget
4. floor plan
5. contractor
6. electrical hazard
7. wiring
8. bricklayer
A. **call in** sick

What do you see in the pictures?

1. How many workers are there? How many are working?

2. Why did two workers call in sick?

3. What is dangerous at the construction site?

 Read the story.

A Bad Day at Work

Sam Lopez is the <u>contractor</u> for a new building. He makes the schedule and supervises the <u>budget</u>. He also solves problems. Today there are a lot of problems.

Two <u>bricklayers</u> <u>called in sick</u> this morning. So Sam has only one bricklayer at work. One hour later, a construction worker fell. He had to go to the <u>clinic</u>.

Construction work is <u>dangerous</u>. Sam always tells his workers to be careful. Yesterday he told them about the new <u>wiring</u> on the site. It's an <u>electrical hazard</u>.

Right now, the building owner is in Sam's office. Her new <u>floor plan</u> has 25 more offices. Sam has a headache. Maybe he needs to call in sick tomorrow.

Reread the story.

1. Make a timeline of the events in this story. What happened first? next? last?

2. Find the sentence "He had to go to the clinic" in paragraph 2. Is "he" the worker or Sam? How do you know?

What do you think?

3. Give examples of good reasons (or excuses) to give when you can't come in to work. Give an example of a bad excuse. Why is it bad?

4. Imagine you are Sam. What do you tell the building owner? Why?

199

Schools and Subjects

1. preschool / nursery school

2. elementary school

3. middle school / junior high school

4. high school

5. career and technical school / vocational school

6. community college

7. college / university

8. adult school

Listen and point. Take turns.

A: *Point to the preschool.*

B: *Point to the high school.*

A: *Point to the adult school.*

Dictate to your partner. Take turns.

A: *Write preschool.*

B: *Is that p-r-e-s-c-h-o-o-l?*

A: *Yes, that's right.*

9 How does Ishmael see the whale?

It's evil.

But here it says …

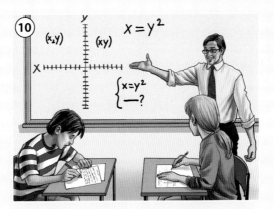

10 $x = y^2$

(x,y) (x,y)

$\begin{cases} x = y^2 \\ \text{—?} \end{cases}$

11 $H_2O \rightarrow$

12 US Civil War
1861-1865
Reasons for the war:

A —
B —
C —

9. language arts

10. math

11. science

12. history

13. world languages

14. English language instruction

15. arts

16. music

17. physical education

13

Muy bien!

GENTE COSAS
estudiante   lápiz

很好

人
学生   物   铅笔

14

Good work!

PEOPLE THINGS
student   pencil

15

16

17

More vocabulary

core course: a subject students have to take.
Math is a core course.

elective: a subject students choose to take. Art is an elective.

Pair practice. Make new conversations.

A: *I go to a community college.*
B: *What subjects are you taking?*
A: *I'm taking history and science.*

English Composition

(1)

factory

1. word

(2)

I worked in a factory.

2. sentence

(3)

Little by little, work and success came to me. My first job wasn't good. I worked in a small factory. Now, I help manage two factories.

3. paragraph

(4)

4. essay

Parts of an Essay

5. title

6. introduction

7. evidence

8. body

9. conclusion

10. quotation

11. citation

12. footnote

13. source

Carlos Lopez
Eng. Comp.
10/03/16

(5) Success in the U.S.

(6) I came to Los Angeles from Mexico in 2006. I had no job, no friends, and no family here. I was homesick and scared, but I did not go home. I took English classes (always at night) and I studied hard. I believed in my future success!

(7) According to the U.S. Census, more than 400,000 new immigrants come to the U.S. every year.[1] Most of us need to find work. During my first year here, my routine was the same: get up; look for work; go to class; go to bed. I had to take jobs with long hours and low pay. Often I had two or three jobs.

(8) Little by little, work and success came to me. My first job wasn't good. I worked in a small factory. Now, I help manage two factories.

(9) Hard work makes success possible, and **(10)** "men were born to succeed, not to fail" (Thoreau, 1853). **(11)** My story demonstrates the truth of that statement.

(12) [1] U.S. Census, 2015 **(13)**

Punctuation

. 14. period

? 15. question mark

! 16. exclamation mark / exclamation point

, 17. comma

" " 18. quotation marks

' 19. apostrophe

: 20. colon

; 21. semicolon

( ) 22. parentheses

- 23. hyphen

Writing Rules

A

Carlos

Mexico

Los Angeles

A. **Capitalize** names.

B

Hard work makes success possible.

B. **Capitalize** the first letter in a sentence.

C

I was homesick and scared, but I did not go home.

C. **Use** punctuation.

D

I came to Los Angeles from Mexico in 2006. I had no job, no friends, and no family here. I was homesick and scared, but I did not go home. I took English classes (always at night) and I studied hard. I believed in my future success!

D. **Indent** the first sentence in a paragraph.

Ways to ask for suggestions on your compositions

What do you think of this title?

Is this paragraph OK? Is the punctuation correct?

Do you have any suggestions for the conclusion?

Pair practice. Make new conversations.

A: *What do you think of this title?*

B: *I think you need to revise it.*

A: *Thanks. How would you revise it?*

The Writing Process

E. **Think about** the assignment.

F. **Brainstorm** ideas.

G. **Organize** your ideas.

H. **Write** a first draft.

I. **Edit.** / **Proofread.**

J. **Revise.** / **Rewrite.**

K. **Get** feedback.

L. **Write** a final draft.

M. **Turn in / Hand in** your paper.

Survey your class. Record the responses.

1. Do you prefer to write essays or read them?
2. Which is more difficult: writing a first draft or revising?

Report: _Five people I surveyed said ___._

Think about it. Discuss.

1. What are interesting topics for essays?
2. Do you like to read quotations? Why or why not?
3. In which jobs are writing skills important?

Mathematics

Integers

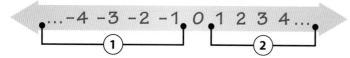

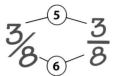

1. negative integers

2. positive integers

Fractions

3. $1, 3, 5, 7, 9, 11 \ldots$

4. $2, 4, 6, 8, 10 \ldots$

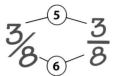

3. odd numbers

4. even numbers

5. numerator

6. denominator

Math Operations

A. **add**   B. **subtract**   C. **multiply**   D. **divide**

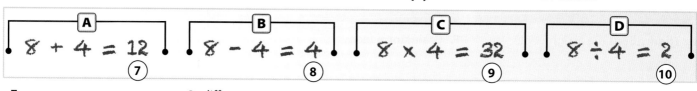

$$8 + 4 = 12 \qquad 8 - 4 = 4 \qquad 8 \times 4 = 32 \qquad 8 \div 4 = 2$$

7. sum

8. difference

9. product

10. quotient

A Math Problem

11.

Tom is 10 years older than Kim. Next year he will be twice as old as Kim. How old is Tom this year?

12.

x = Kim's age now
$x + 10$ = Tom's age now
$x + 1$ = Kim's age next year
$2(x + 1)$ = Tom's age next year

$x + 10 + 1 = 2(x + 1)$
$x + 11 = 2x + 2$
$11 - 2 = 2x - x$ 13.

$x = 9$, Kim is 9, Tom is 19   14.

15.

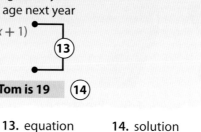

horizontal axis

vertical axis

11. word problem

12. variable   13. equation   14. solution   15. graph

Types of Math

16.

How much are they?

$79 NOW 40% OFF!

x = the sale price
$x = 79.00 - .40 (79.00)$
$x = \$47.40$

16. algebra

17.

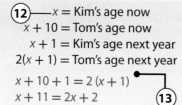

How many do I need?

area of path = 24 square ft.
area of brick = 2 square ft.
$24 / 2 = 12$ bricks

17. geometry

18.

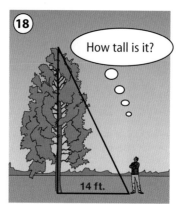

How tall is it?

14 ft.

$\tan 63° = \text{height} / 14 \text{ feet}$
$\text{height} = 14 \text{ feet} (\tan 63°)$
$\text{height} \approx 27.48 \text{ feet}$

18. trigonometry

19.

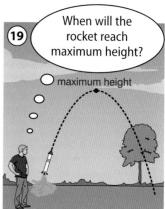

When will the rocket reach maximum height?

maximum height

$s(t) = -\frac{1}{2} g t^2 + V_0 t + h$
$s'(t) = -g t + V_0 = 0$
$t = V_0 / g$

19. calculus

204

Name: _Jennifer Lovo_

Date: _17/09/15_

◇
◆
◇

A. Look at pages 40–41. Listen to two people talk about family photos. Listen to the entire conversation. Answer the questions with your class.

1. Who is the woman?

2. Who is the man?

3. Is there a picture of the man on page 40 or page 41?

B. Close your book. Listen to each part of the conversation. Write the years you hear.

1. We went to Egypt in _2005_.

2. He was born in _1935_, two years before me.

3. He immigrated with his parents in _1950_.

4. He graduated in _1963_.

5. He got his degree in _1959_.

Lines

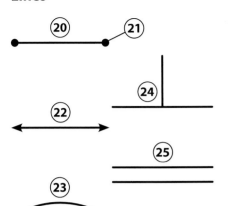

20. line segment

21. endpoint

22. straight line

23. curved line

24. perpendicular lines

25. parallel lines

Angles

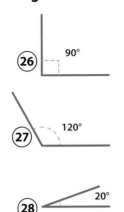

26. right angle / 90° angle

27. obtuse angle

28. acute angle

Shapes

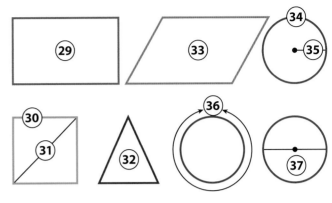

29. rectangle

30. square

31. diagonal

32. triangle

33. parallelogram

34. circle

35. radius

36. circumference

37. diameter

Geometric Solids

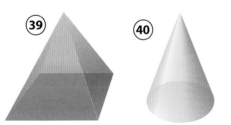

38. cube

39. pyramid

40. cone

41. cylinder

42. sphere

Measuring Area and Volume

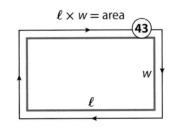

$\ell \times w = $ area

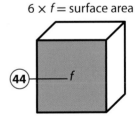

$6 \times f = $ surface area

43. perimeter

44. face

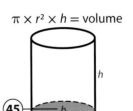

$\pi \times r^2 \times h = $ volume

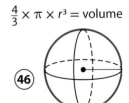

$\frac{4}{3} \times \pi \times r^3 = $ volume

$\pi \approx 3.14$

45. base

46. pi

Survey your class. Record the responses.

1. Is division easy or difficult?
2. Is algebra easy or difficult?

Report: _50% of the class thinks ____ is difficult._

Think about it. Discuss.

1. What's the best way to learn mathematics?
2. How can you find the area of your classroom?
3. Which jobs use math? Which don't?

Biology

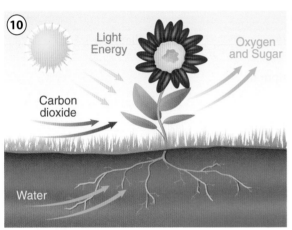  

1. organisms

2. biologist

3. slide

4. cell

5. cell wall

6. cell membrane

7. nucleus

8. chromosome

9. cytoplasm

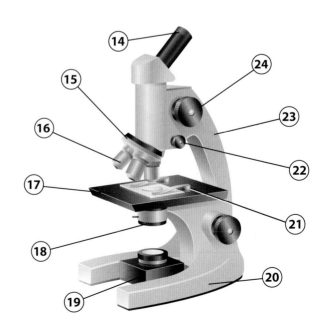

Light Energy

Carbon dioxide

Oxygen and Sugar

Water

THE DESERT

THE OCEAN

10. photosynthesis

11. habitat

12. vertebrates

13. invertebrates

A Microscope

14. eyepiece

15. revolving nosepiece

16. objective

17. stage

18. diaphragm

19. light source

20. base

21. stage clips

22. fine adjustment knob

23. arm

24. coarse adjustment knob

Chemistry

25. chemist

26. periodic table

27. molecule

28. atom

29. nucleus

30. electron

31. proton

32. neutron

33. physicist

Physics

34. formula

35. prism

36. magnet

A Science Lab

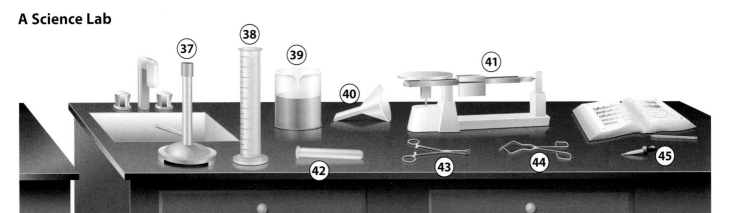

37. Bunsen burner

38. graduated cylinder

39. beaker

40. funnel

41. balance / scale

42. test tube

43. forceps

44. crucible tongs

45. dropper

An Experiment

A. **State** a hypothesis.

Salt and sugar crystals will grow the same way.

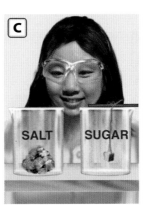

B. **Do** an experiment.

C. **Observe.**

D. **Record** the results.

E. **Draw** a conclusion.

Salt crystals grow faster than sugar crystals.

U.S. History

Colonial Period

1. thirteen colonies

2. colonists

3. Native American

4. slaves

5. Declaration of Independence

6. First Continental Congress

7. founders

8. Revolutionary War

9. redcoat

10. minuteman

11. first president

12. Constitution

13. Bill of Rights

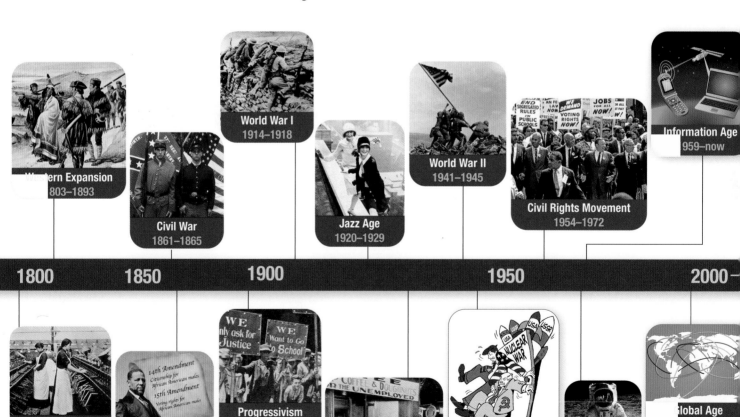

Western Expansion
1803–1893

Civil War
1861–1865

World War I
1914–1918

Jazz Age
1920–1929

World War II
1941–1945

Civil Rights Movement
1954–1972

Information Age
1959–now

Industrial Revolution
1793–1908

1st African American senator: H. Revels
Reconstruction
1865–1877

Progressivism
1889–1916

Great Depression
1929–1941

Cold War
1945–1989

Space Age
1958–now

Global Age
1994–now

1800   1850   1900   1950   2000

Civilizations

Pyramids

Parthenon

1

2

Times Square

Julius Caesar

3

Qin Shi Huang

King Sobhuza II

4

Queen Elizabeth I

5

Benito Juárez

6

Benito Mussolini

7

Shinzo Abe

1. ancient

2. modern

3. emperor

4. monarch

5. president

6. dictator

7. prime minister

Historical Terms

8

9

Vikings

Astronauts

8. exploration

9. explorer

10

11

10. war

11. army

12

13

12. immigration

13. immigrant

14

15

Wolfgang Mozart

Duke Ellington

14. composer

15. composition

16

17

Susan B. Anthony

César Chávez

16. political movement

17. activist

18

19

Thomas Edison

Guillermo Camarena

18. inventor

19. invention

Creating a Document

A. **open** the program

B. **create** a new document

C. **type**

D. **save** the document

E. **close** the document

F. **quit** the program

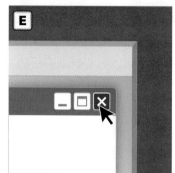

Selecting and Changing Text

G. **click** on the screen

H. **double-click** to select a word

I. **delete** a word

J. **drag** to select text

K. **copy** text

L. **paste** text

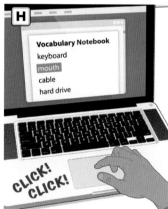

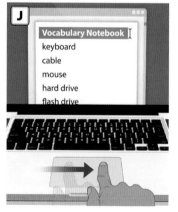

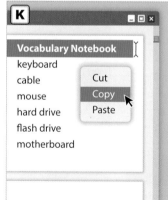

More vocabulary

keyboard shortcut: use of the keys on the keyboard to cut, copy, paste, etc. For example, press "control" on a PC ("Command" on a Mac) and "C" to copy text.

Identify Diego's problem. Brainstorm solutions.

Diego is nervous around computers. He needs to complete an online job application. His brother, Luis, offers to apply for him. What could Diego do?

Moving around the Screen

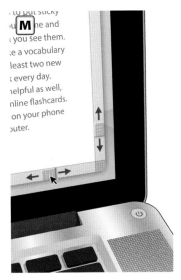

M. scroll

N. use the arrow keys

O. create a username

Registering an Account

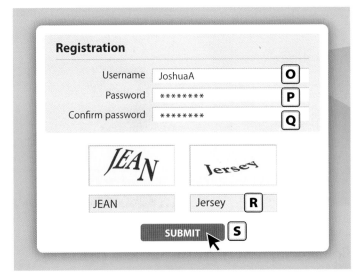

P. create a password

Q. reenter the password / **type** the password again

R. type the verification code

S. click submit

Sending Email

T. log in to your account

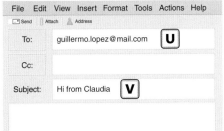

U. address the email

V. type the subject

W. compose / **write** the message

X. check your spelling

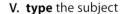

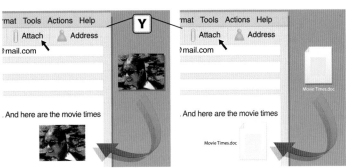

Y. attach a file

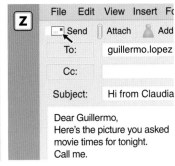

Z. send the email

Internet Research

1. research question
2. search engine
3. search box
4. keywords
5. search results
6. links

Conducting Research

A. **select** a search engine

B. **type** in a phrase

C. **type** in a question

D. **click** the search icon / **search**

E. **look** at the results

F. **click** on a link

G. **bookmark** a site

H. **keep** a record of sources

I. **cite** sources

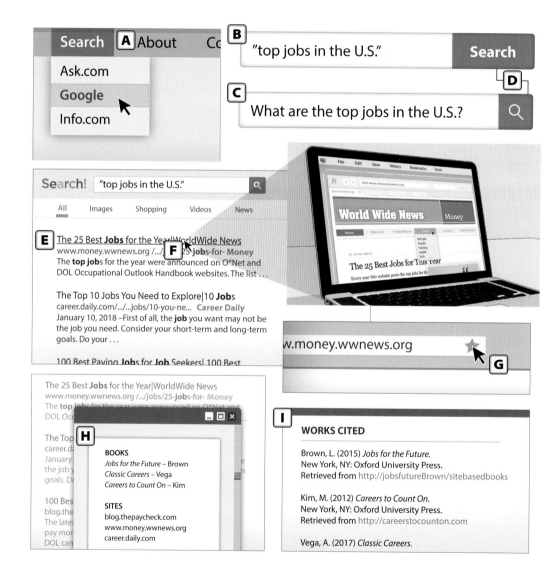

More vocabulary

research: to search for and record information that answers a question

investigate: to research a problem or situation

Ways to talk about your research

My research shows _____.
According to my research, _____.
These are the results of my research: _____.

8. browser window

9. back button

10. URL / website address

11. refresh button

12. web page

13. source

14. tab

15. drop-down menu

16. content

17. pop-up ad

18. video player

19. social media links

20. date

File   Edit   View   History   Bookmarks   Tools

www.money.wwnews.org

www.money.org

World Wide News | Money

Home   Retirement   Personal Finance   Career   Investing   Estate Planning

Best pay
Popular
Training
Health
Tech

BY JOHN SMITH

The 25 Best Jobs for This Year

Every year this website posts the top jobs for the
popularity is calculated based on its projected g
next five years, associated salary, number of yea
tion and training required, and a satisfaction su
Tristan Mathes & Associates.

While it is tempting to make career decisions ba
100 list, it is important to remember that these
only part of the picture.

Click to continue reading

Buy it NOW!!

JANUARY 8, 2017 7:00 PM EST

Internet Research: online practice

Type "practice" in the search bar. Add more keywords.
("ESL vocabulary," etc.)

Report: *I found <u>vocabulary</u> practice on a site called ____.*

Think about it. Discuss.

1. Which is better for Internet research: searching with a
   question, a phrase, or keywords? Explain.
2. Do you enjoy research? Why or why not?

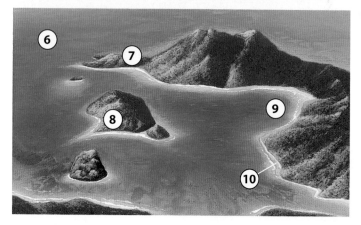

1. rain forest

2. waterfall

3. river

4. desert

5. sand dune

6. ocean

7. peninsula

8. island

9. bay

10. beach

11. forest

12. shore

13. lake

14. mountain peak

15. mountain range

16. hills

17. canyon

18. valley

19. plains

20. meadow

21. pond

More vocabulary

body of water: a river, a lake, or an ocean
stream / creek: a very small river
inhabitants: the people and animals living in a habitat

Survey your class. Record the responses.

1. Would you rather live by the ocean or a lake?
2. Would you rather live in a desert or a rainforest?
Report: *Fifteen of us would rather _____ than _____.*

The Solar System and the Planets

1. Mercury
2. Venus
3. Earth
4. Mars
5. Jupiter
6. Saturn
7. Uranus
8. Neptune

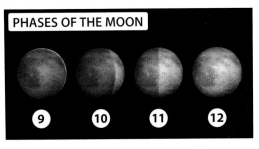

PHASES OF THE MOON

SPACE

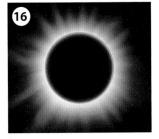

9. new moon
10. crescent moon
11. quarter moon
12. full moon
13. star
14. constellation
15. galaxy
16. solar eclipse

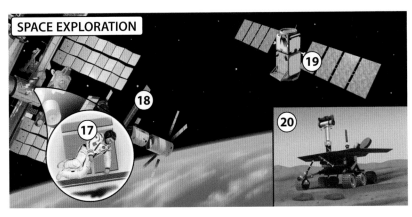

SPACE EXPLORATION

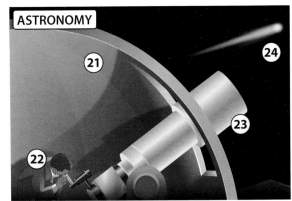

ASTRONOMY

17. astronaut
18. space station
19. satellite
20. probe / rover
21. observatory
22. astronomer
23. telescope
24. comet

More vocabulary

lunar eclipse: when the moon is in the earth's shadow
Big Dipper: a famous part of the constellation Ursa Major
Sirius: the brightest star in the night sky

Think about it. Discuss.

1. Do you want to travel in space? Why or why not?
2. Who should pay for space exploration? Why?
3. What do you like best about the night sky?

215

Trees and Plants

PARTS OF A TREE

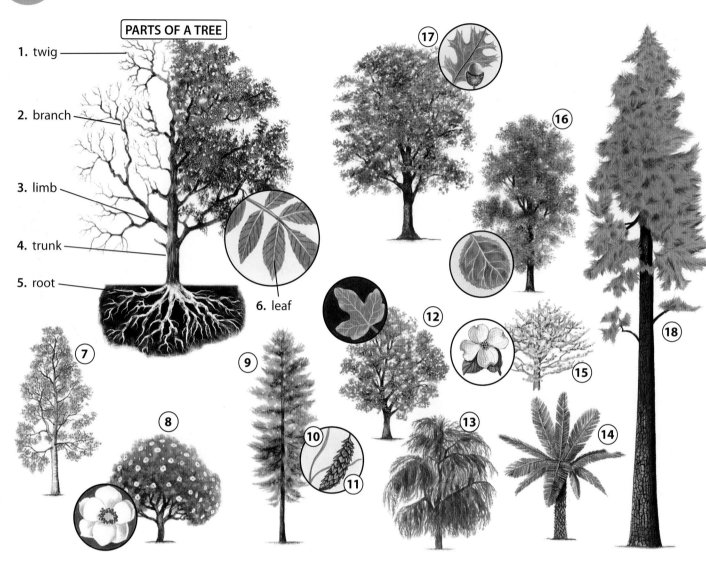

1. twig
2. branch
3. limb
4. trunk
5. root
6. leaf

7. birch
8. magnolia
9. pine
10. needle
11. pine cone
12. maple
13. willow
14. palm
15. dogwood
16. elm
17. oak
18. redwood

Plants

19. holly
20. berries
21. cactus
22. vine
23. poison sumac
24. poison oak
25. poison ivy

Parts of a Flower

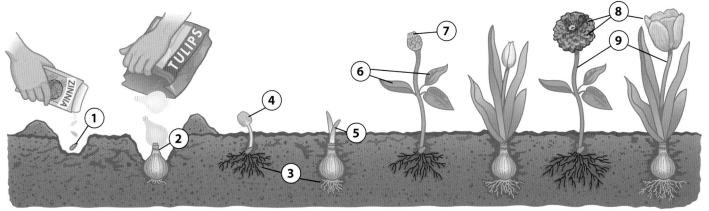

1. seed
2. bulb
3. roots

4. seedling
5. shoot
6. leaves

7. bud
8. petals
9. stems

10. sunflower
11. tulip
12. hibiscus
13. marigold
14. daisy

15. rose
16. iris
17. crocus
18. gardenia
19. orchid

20. carnation
21. chrysanthemum
22. jasmine
23. violet
24. poinsettia

25. daffodil
26. lily
27. houseplant
28. bouquet
29. thorn

Sea Animals

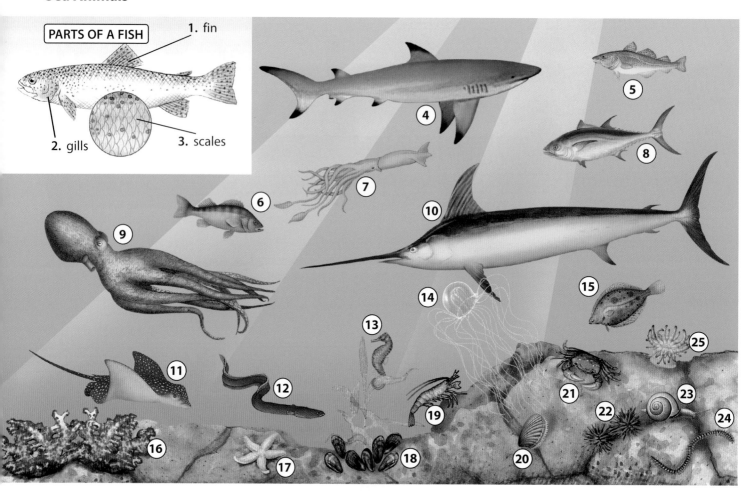

PARTS OF A FISH

1. fin
2. gills
3. scales

4. shark	**9.** octopus	**14.** jellyfish	**19.** shrimp	**24.** worm
5. cod	**10.** swordfish	**15.** flounder	**20.** scallop	**25.** sea anemone
6. bass	**11.** ray	**16.** coral	**21.** crab	
7. squid	**12.** eel	**17.** starfish	**22.** sea urchin	
8. tuna	**13.** seahorse	**18.** mussel	**23.** snail	

Amphibians

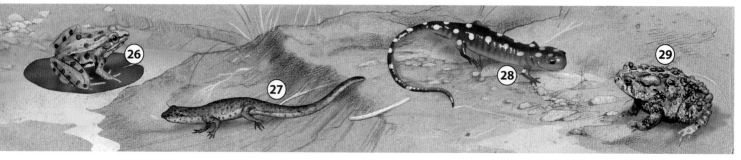

26. frog   **27.** newt   **28.** salamander   **29.** toad

Sea Mammals

30. water

31. dolphin

32. porpoise

33. whale

34. walrus

35. sea lion

36. seal

37. sea otter

38. rock

Reptiles

39. alligator

40. crocodile

41. tortoise

42. turtle

43. lizard

44. cobra

45. rattlesnake

46. garter snake

Birds, Insects, and Arachnids

PARTS OF A BIRD

1. wing
2. claw
3. beak / bill
4. feather

5. nest	8. sparrow	11. hummingbird	14. goose	17. robin
6. owl	9. woodpecker	12. penguin	15. peacock	
7. blue jay	10. eagle	13. duck	16. pigeon	

Insects and Arachnids

18. wasp	22. moth	26. honeybee	30. spider
19. beetle	23. mosquito	27. ladybug	31. scorpion
20. butterfly	24. cricket	28. tick	
21. caterpillar	25. grasshopper	29. fly	

Farm Animals / Livestock

1. cow
2. pig
3. donkey
4. horse
5. goat
6. sheep
7. rooster
8. hen

Pets

9. cat
10. kitten
11. dog
12. puppy
13. rabbit
14. guinea pig
15. parakeet
16. goldfish

Rodents

17. rat
18. mouse
19. gopher
20. chipmunk
21. squirrel
22. prairie dog

More vocabulary

Farm animals and pets are **domesticated**. They work for and/or live with people. Animals that are not domesticated are **wild**. Most rodents are wild.

Survey your class. Record the responses.

1. Have you worked with farm animals? Which ones?
2. Are you afraid of rodents? Which ones?

Report: _Lee_ has worked with _cows_. _He's_ afraid of _rats_.

221

Mammals

1. moose
2. mountain lion
3. coyote
4. opossum

5. wolf
6. buffalo / bison
7. bat
8. armadillo

9. beaver
10. porcupine
11. bear
12. skunk

13. raccoon
14. deer
15. fox

16. antlers
17. hooves

18. whiskers
19. coat / fur

20. paw
21. horn

22. tail
23. quill

24. anteater	**29.** gorilla	**34.** leopard	**39.** orangutan	**44.** kangaroo
25. llama	**30.** hyena	**35.** antelope	**40.** panther	**45.** koala
26. monkey	**31.** baboon	**36.** lion	**41.** panda	**46.** platypus
27. chimpanzee	**32.** giraffe	**37.** tiger	**42.** elephant	
28. rhinoceros	**33.** zebra	**38.** camel	**43.** hippopotamus	

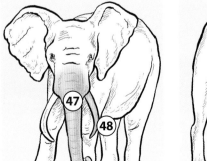

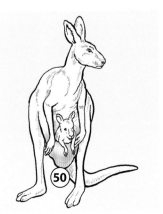

47. trunk   **48.** tusk   **49.** mane   **50.** pouch   **51.** hump

223

Energy and the Environment

Energy Sources

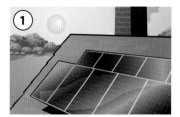

1. solar energy

2. wind power

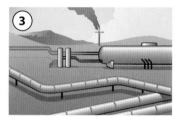

3. natural gas

4. coal

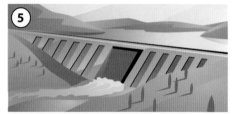

5. hydroelectric power

6. oil / petroleum

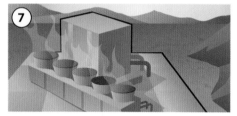

7. geothermal energy

8. nuclear energy

9. biomass / bioenergy

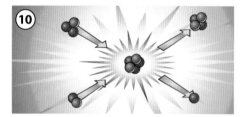

10. fusion

Pollution

11. air pollution / smog

12. hazardous waste

13. acid rain

14. water pollution

15. radiation

16. pesticide poisoning

17. oil spill

More vocabulary

Environmental Protection Agency (EPA): the federal group that responds to pollution and environmental disasters

Internet Research: recycling

Type "recycle" and your city in the search bar. Look for information on local recycling centers.
Report: *You can recycle <u>cans</u> at _____.*

Ways to Conserve Energy and Resources

A. **reduce** trash

B. **reuse** shopping bags

C. **recycle**

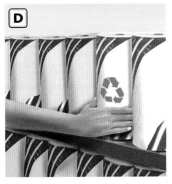

D. **buy** recycled products

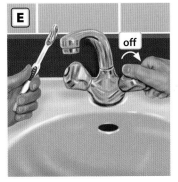

E. **save** water

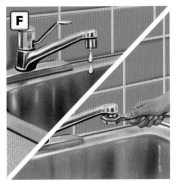

F. **fix** leaky faucets

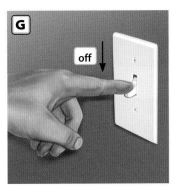

G. **turn off** lights

H. **use** energy-efficient bulbs

I. **carpool**

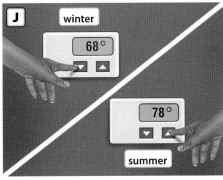

J. **adjust** the thermostat

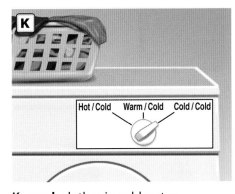

K. **wash** clothes in cold water

L. **don't litter**

M. **compost** food scraps

N. **plant** a tree

A Graduation

Home | **Search** | **Invite** | **Mail** |

All Adelia's photos

I loved Art History.

My last economics lesson

Marching Band is great!

The photographer was upset.

We look good!

I get my diploma.

Dad and his digital camera

1. photographer	3. serious photo	5. podium	7. cap	A. **take** a picture	C. **celebrate**
2. funny photo	4. guest speaker	6. ceremony	8. gown	B. **cry**	

Videos | Music | Classifieds |

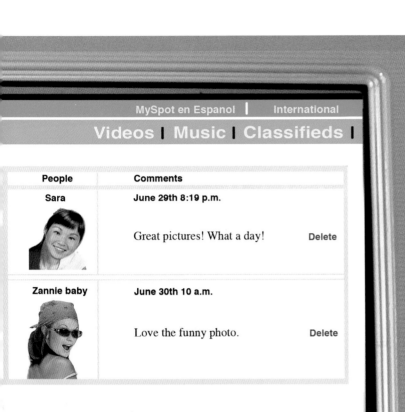

People	Comments	
Sara	**June 29th 8:19 p.m.**	
	Great pictures! What a day!	Delete
Zannie baby	**June 30th 10 a.m.**	
	Love the funny photo.	Delete

I'm behind the mayor.

We're all very happy.

What do you see in the pictures?

1. Which classes are Adelia's favorites?
2. Do you prefer the funny or the serious graduation photo? Why?
3. Who is standing at the podium?
4. What are the graduates throwing in the air? Why?

Read the story.

A Graduation

Look at these great photos on my web page! The first three are from my favorite classes, but the other pictures are from graduation day.

There are two pictures of my classmates in <u>caps</u> and <u>gowns</u>. In the first picture, we're laughing and the <u>photographer</u> is upset. In the second photo, we're serious. I like the <u>serious photo</u>, but I love the <u>funny photo</u>!

There's also a picture of our <u>guest speaker</u>, the mayor. She is standing at the <u>podium</u>. Next, you can see me at the graduation <u>ceremony</u>. My dad wanted to <u>take a picture</u> of me with my diploma. That's my mom next to him. She <u>cries</u> when she's happy.

After the ceremony, everyone was happy, but no one cried. We wanted to <u>celebrate</u> and we did!

Reread the story.

1. Which events happened before the graduation? After?
2. Why does the author say, "but no one cried" in paragraph 4?

What do you think?

3. What kinds of ceremonies are important for children? for teens? for adults?

Places to Go

1. zoo

2. movies

3. botanical garden

4. bowling alley

5. rock concert

6. swap meet /
   flea market

7. aquarium

Places to Go in Our City

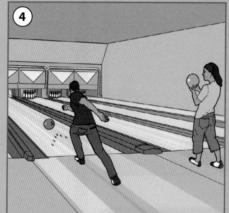

Listen and point. Take turns.

A: *Point to the <u>zoo</u>.*
B: *Point to the <u>flea market</u>.*
A: *Point to the <u>rock concert</u>.*

Dictate to your partner. Take turns.

A: *Write these words: <u>zoo, movies, aquarium</u>.*
B: *<u>Zoo, movies</u>, and what?*
A: *And <u>aquarium</u>.*

8. play

9. art museum

10. amusement park

11. opera

12. nightclub

13. county fair

14. classical concert

Ways to make plans using *Let's go*

Let's go to <u>the amusement park</u> tomorrow.

Let's go to <u>the opera</u> on Saturday.

Let's go to <u>the movies</u> tonight.

Pair practice. Make new conversations.

A: <u>Let's go to the zoo this afternoon</u>.

B: *OK. And let's go to* <u>the movies tonight</u>.

A: *That sounds like a good plan.*

229

The Park and Playground

1. ball field	**5.** fountain	**9.** water fountain	**13.** slide
2. cyclist	**6.** tennis court	**10.** bench	**14.** climbing apparatus
3. bike path	**7.** skateboard	**11.** swings	**15.** sandbox
4. jump rope	**8.** picnic table	**12.** tricycle	**16.** outdoor grill

A. **pull** the wagon

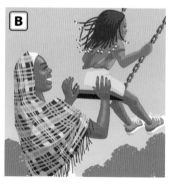

B. **push** the swing

C. **climb** the bars

D. **picnic / have** a picnic

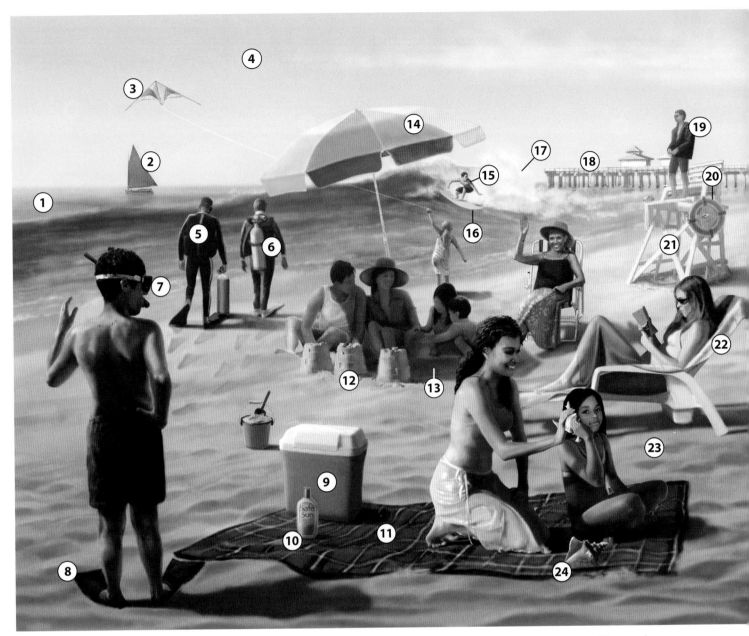

1. ocean / water
2. sailboat
3. kite
4. sky
5. wetsuit
6. scuba tank

7. diving mask
8. fins
9. cooler
10. sunscreen / sunblock
11. blanket
12. sandcastle

13. shade
14. beach umbrella
15. surfer
16. surfboard
17. wave
18. pier

19. lifeguard
20. lifesaving device
21. lifeguard station
22. beach chair
23. sand
24. seashell

More vocabulary

seaweed: a plant that grows in the ocean
tide: the level of the ocean. The tide goes in and out every 12 hours.

Grammar Point: prepositions *in, on, under*

*Where are the little kids? They're **under** the umbrella.*
*Where's the cooler? It's **on** the blanket.*
*Where's the kite? It's **in** the sky.*

1. boating

2. rafting

3. canoeing

4. fishing

5. camping

6. backpacking

7. hiking

8. mountain biking

9. horseback riding

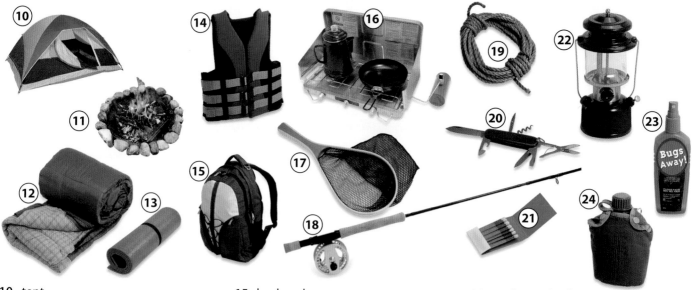

10. tent

11. campfire

12. sleeping bag

13. foam pad

14. life vest

15. backpack

16. camping stove

17. fishing net

18. fishing pole

19. rope

20. multi-use knife

21. matches

22. lantern

23. insect repellent

24. canteen

1. downhill skiing

2. snowboarding

3. cross-country skiing

4. ice skating

5. figure skating

6. sledding

7. waterskiing

8. sailing

9. surfing

10. windsurfing

11. snorkeling

12. scuba diving

More vocabulary

speed skating: racing while ice skating
kitesurfing: surfing with a small surfboard and a kite

Internet Research: popular winter sports

Type "popular winter sports" in the search bar.
Compare the information on two sites.
Report: *Two sites said _____ is a popular winter sport.*

1. archery

2. billiards / pool

3. bowling

4. boxing

5. cycling / biking

6. badminton

7. fencing

8. golf

9. gymnastics

10. inline skating

11. martial arts

12. racquetball

13. skateboarding

14. table tennis

15. tennis

16. weightlifting

17. wrestling

18. track and field

19. horse racing

Pair practice. Make new conversations.

A: *What sports do you like?*

B: *I like <u>bowling</u>. What do you like?*

A: *I like <u>gymnastics</u>.*

Internet Research: dangerous sports

Type "most dangerous sports" in the search bar.
Look for information on two or more sites.

Report: *According to my research, ____ is dangerous.*

1. score	**3.** team	**5.** player	**7.** basketball court
2. coach	**4.** fan	**6.** official / referee	**8.** basketball hoop

9. basketball

10. baseball

11. softball

12. football

13. soccer

14. ice hockey

15. volleyball

16. water polo

More vocabulary

win: to have the best score
lose: the opposite of win
tie: to have the same score

captain: the team leader
goalie: the team member who protects the goal in soccer, ice hockey, and water polo
umpire: the referee in baseball
Little League: a baseball and softball program for children

Sports Verbs

A. pitch

B. hit

C. throw

D. catch

E. kick

F. tackle

G. pass

H. shoot

I. jump

J. dribble

K. dive

L. swim

M. stretch

N. exercise / work out

O. bend

P. serve

Q. swing

R. start

S. race

T. finish

U. skate

V. ski

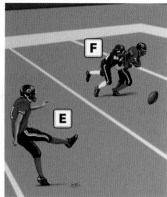

Use the new words.
Look at page 235. Name the actions you see.

A: He's <u>throwing</u>.
B: She's <u>jumping</u>.

Ways to talk about your sports skills

I can <u>throw</u>, but I can't <u>catch</u>.
I <u>swim</u> well, but I don't <u>dive</u> well.
I'm good at <u>skating</u>, but I'm terrible at <u>skiing</u>.

1. golf club	8. arrows	15. catcher's mask	22. weights
2. tennis racket	9. ice skates	16. uniform	23. snowboard
3. volleyball	10. inline skates	17. glove	24. skis
4. basketball	11. hockey stick	18. baseball	25. ski poles
5. bowling ball	12. soccer ball	19. football helmet	26. ski boots
6. bow	13. shin guards	20. shoulder pads	27. flying disc*
7. target	14. baseball bat	21. football	*Note: one brand is Frisbee®, of Wham-O, Inc.

Use the new words.
Look at pages 234–235. Name the sports equipment you see.

A: *Those are ice skates.*
B: *That's a football.*

Survey your class. Record the responses.
1. What sports equipment do you own?
2. What sports stores do you recommend?
Report: *Sam* owns a ____. *He* recommends ____.

A. **collect** things   B. **play** games   C. **quilt**   D. **do** crafts

Collectibles

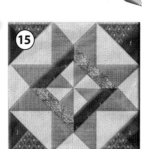

1. figurine	5. board game	9. model kit	13. construction paper
2. baseball cards	6. dice	10. acrylic paint	14. woodworking kit
3. video game console	7. checkers	11. glue stick	15. quilt block
4. video game controller	8. chess	12. glue gun	16. rotary cutter

Grammar Point: *used to*

*When I was a kid, I **used to** play cards every day.*
Now, I don't play very often.

Pair practice. Make new conversations.

A: *What were your hobbies when you were a kid?*
B: *I used to <u>collect baseball cards</u>. And you?*
A: *I used to <u>play video games</u>.*

E. paint   **F. knit**   **G. pretend**   **H. play** cards

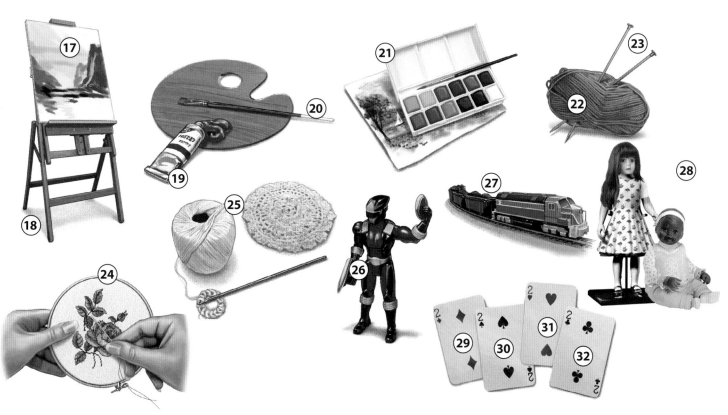

17. canvas	21. watercolors	25. crochet	29. diamonds
18. easel	22. yarn	26. action figure	30. spades
19. oil paint	23. knitting needles	27. model train	31. hearts
20. paintbrush	24. embroidery	28. dolls	32. clubs

Ways to talk about hobbies and games

*This <u>board game</u> is **interesting**. It makes me think.*
*That <u>video game</u> is **boring**. Nothing happens.*
*I love to <u>play cards</u>. It's **fun** to play with my friends.*

Internet Research: popular hobbies

Type "most popular hobbies" in the search bar.
Look for information on one or more sites.
Report: *I read that _____ is a popular hobby.*

239

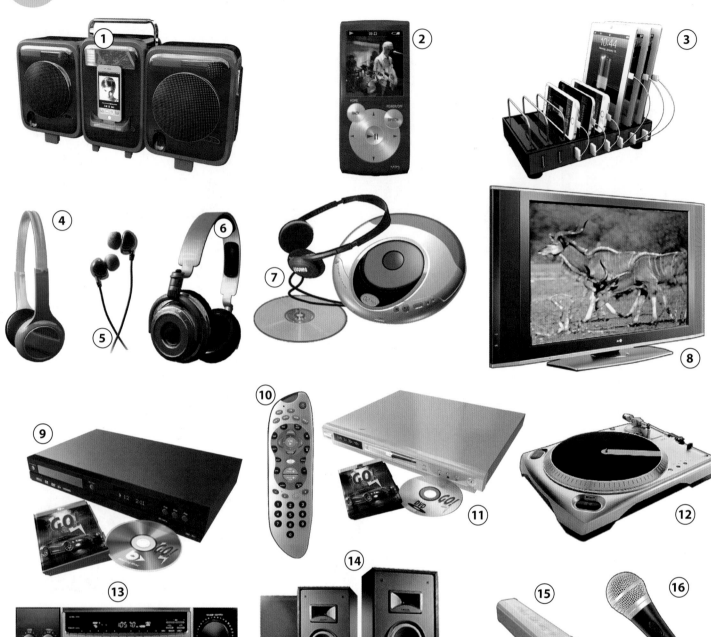

1. boom box

2. video MP3 player

3. dock / charging station

4. lightweight headphones

5. earbuds / in-ear headphones

6. noise-canceling headphones

7. personal CD player

8. flat-screen TV / flat-panel TV

9. Blu-ray player

10. universal remote

11. DVD player

12. turntable

13. tuner

14. speakers

15. portable charger

16. microphone

17. digital camera

18. memory card

19. zoom lens

20. tripod

21. camcorder

22. camera case / bag

23. battery pack

24. battery charger

25. plug

26. international power adapter

27. LCD projector

28. screen

29. photo album

30. digital photo album

31. out of focus

32. overexposed

33. underexposed

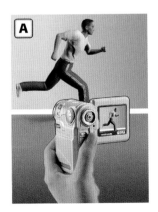

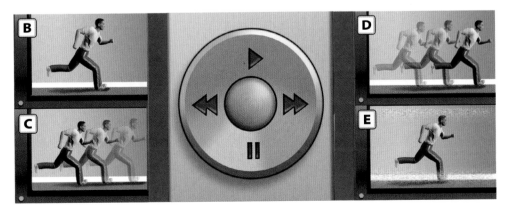

A. record

B. play

C. rewind

D. fast forward

E. pause

241

Types of TV Programs

1. news program

2. sitcom (situation comedy)

3. cartoon

4. talk show

5. soap opera

6. reality show

7. nature program

8. game show

9. children's program

10. shopping program

11. sports program

12. drama

Types of Movies

13. comedy

14. tragedy

15. western

16. romance

17. horror story

18. science fiction story

19. action story / adventure story

20. mystery / suspense

Types of Music

21. classical

22. blues

23. rock

24. jazz

25. pop

26. hip-hop

27. country

28. R&B / soul

29. folk

30. gospel

31. reggae

32. world music

A. play an instrument

B. sing a song

C. conduct an orchestra

D. be in a rock band

Woodwinds

1. flute
2. clarinet
3. oboe
4. bassoon
5. saxophone

Strings

6. violin
7. cello
8. bass
9. guitar

Brass

10. trombone
11. trumpet / horn
12. tuba
13. French horn

Percussion

14. piano
15. xylophone
16. drums
17. tambourine

Other Instruments

18. electric keyboard
19. accordion
20. organ
21. harmonica

1. parade	**6.** heart	**11.** costume	**15.** ornament
2. float	**7.** fireworks	**12.** candy	**16.** Christmas tree
3. confetti	**8.** flag	**13.** feast	**17.** candy cane
4. couple	**9.** mask	**14.** turkey	**18.** string lights
5. card	**10.** jack-o'-lantern		

*Thanksgiving is on the fourth Thursday in November.

A Birthday Party

1. decorations
2. deck
3. present / gift

A. **videotape**
B. **make** a wish
C. **blow out**
D. **hide**
E. **bring**
F. **wrap**

Happy Birthday!

What do you see in the picture?

1. What kinds of decorations do you see?

2. What are people doing at this birthday party?

3. What wish did the teenager make?

4. How many presents did people bring?

Read the story.

A Birthday Party

Today is Lou and Gani Bombata's birthday barbecue. There are <u>decorations</u> around the backyard, and food and drinks on the <u>deck</u>. There are also <u>presents</u>. Everyone in the Bombata family likes to <u>bring</u> presents.

Right now, it's time for cake. Gani <u>is blowing out</u> the candles, and Lou <u>is making a wish</u>. Lou's mom wants to <u>videotape</u> everyone, but she can't find Lou's brother, Todd. Todd hates to sing, so he always <u>hides</u> for the birthday song.

Lou's sister, Amaka, has to <u>wrap</u> some <u>gifts</u>. She doesn't want Lou to see. Amaka isn't worried. She knows her family loves to sing. She can put her gifts on the present table before they finish the first song.

Reread the story.

1. Which paragraph gives you the most information about the Bombata family? Explain why.

2. Tell the story in your own words.

What do you think?

3. What wish do you think Gani made? Give your reasons.

4. Imagine you are invited to this party. You want to get one special gift for Gani *and* Lou to share. What's one gift they could both enjoy?

Verb Guide

Verbs in English are either regular or irregular in the past tense and past participle forms.

Regular Verbs

The regular verbs below are marked 1, 2, 3, or 4 according to four different spelling patterns. (See page 250 for the irregular verbs, which do not follow any of these patterns.)

Spelling Patterns for the Past and the Past Participle	Example	
1. Add -ed to the end of the verb.	ASK	ASKED
2. Add -d to the end of the verb.	LIVE	LIVED
3. Double the final consonant and add -ed to the end of the verb.	DROP	DROPPED
4. Drop the final y and add -ied to the end of the verb.	CRY	CRIED

The Oxford Picture Dictionary List of Regular Verbs

accept (1)
add (1)
address (1)
adjust (1)
agree (2)
answer (1)
apologize (2)
appear (1)
applaud (1)
apply (4)
arrange (2)
arrest (1)
arrive (2)
ask (1)
assemble (2)
assist (1)
attach (1)
attend (1)
bake (2)
bargain (1)
bathe (2)
block (1)
board (1)
boil (1)
bookmark (1)
borrow (1)
bow (1)
brainstorm (1)
breathe (2)
browse (2)
brush (1)
bubble (2)
buckle (2)
burn (1)
bus (1)
calculate (2)
call (1)

capitalize (2)
carpool (1)
carry (4)
cash (1)
celebrate (2)
change (2)
check (1)
chill (1)
choke (2)
chop (3)
circle (2)
cite (2)
claim (1)
clarify (4)
clean (1)
clear (1)
click (1)
climb (1)
close (2)
collate (2)
collect (1)
color (1)
comb (1)
comfort (1)
commit (3)
compare (2)
complain (1)
complete (2)
compliment (1)
compose (2)
compost (1)
conceal (1)
conduct (1)
consult (1)
contact (1)
convert (1)
convict (1)

cook (1)
cooperate (2)
copy (4)
correct (1)
cough (1)
count (1)
create (2)
cross (1)
cry (4)
dance (2)
debate (2)
decline (2)
delete (2)
deliver (1)
design (1)
dial (1)
dice (2)
dictate (2)
die (2)
direct (1)
disagree (2)
discipline (2)
discuss (1)
disinfect (1)
distribute (2)
dive (2)
divide (2)
double-click (1)
drag (3)
dress (1)
dribble (2)
drill (1)
drop (3)
drown (1)
dry (4)
dust (1)
dye (2)

earn (1)
edit (1)
empty (4)
end (1)
enter (1)
erase (2)
evacuate (2)
examine (2)
exchange (2)
exercise (2)
expire (2)
explain (1)
explore (2)
exterminate (2)
fast forward (1)
fasten (1)
fax (1)
fertilize (2)
fill (1)
finish (1)
fix (1)
floss (1)
fold (1)
follow (1)
garden (1)
gargle (2)
graduate (2)
grate (2)
grease (2)
greet (1)
hail (1)
hammer (1)
hand (1)
harvest (1)
help (1)
hire (2)
hug (3)

identify (4)
immigrate (2)
indent (1)
inquire (2)
insert (1)
inspect (1)
install (1)
introduce (2)
investigate (2)
invite (2)
iron (1)
jaywalk (1)
join (1)
jump (1)
kick (1)
kiss (1)
knit (3)
label (1)
land (1)
laugh (1)
learn (1)
lengthen (1)
lift (1)
list (1)
listen (1)
litter (1)
live (2)
load (1)
lock (1)
log (3)
look (1)
mail (1)
manufacture (2)
match (1)
measure (2)
microwave (2)
milk (1)
misbehave (2)
miss (1)
mix (1)
monitor (1)
mop (3)
move (2)
mow (1)
multiply (4)
negotiate (2)
network (1)
numb (1)
nurse (2)

obey (1)
observe (2)
offer (1)
open (1)
operate (2)
order (1)
organize (2)
overdose (2)
pack (1)
paint (1)
park (1)
participate (2)
pass (1)
paste (2)
pause (2)
peel (1)
perm (1)
pick (1)
pitch (1)
plan (3)
plant (1)
play (1)
polish (1)
pour (1)
praise (2)
preheat (1)
prepare (2)
prescribe (2)
press (1)
pretend (1)
print (1)
program (3)
protect (1)
pull (1)
purchase (2)
push (1)
quilt (1)
race (2)
raise (2)
rake (2)
receive (2)
record (1)
recycle (2)
redecorate (2)
reduce (2)
reenter (1)
refuse (2)
register (1)
relax (1)

remain (1)
remove (2)
renew (1)
repair (1)
replace (2)
report (1)
request (1)
research (1)
respond (1)
retire (2)
return (1)
reuse (2)
revise (2)
rinse (2)
rock (1)
sauté (1)
save (2)
scan (3)
schedule (2)
scroll (1)
scrub (3)
search (1)
seat (1)
select (1)
sentence (2)
separate (2)
serve (2)
share (2)
shave (2)
ship (3)
shop (3)
shorten (1)
shower (1)
sign (1)
simmer (1)
skate (2)
ski (1)
slice (2)
smell (1)
smile (2)
smoke (2)
solve (2)
sort (1)
spell (1)
spoon (1)
staple (2)
start (1)
state (2)
stay (1)

steam (1)
stir (3)
stop (3)
stow (1)
stretch (1)
study (4)
submit (3)
subtract (1)
supervise (2)
swallow (1)
tackle (2)
talk (1)
taste (2)
thank (1)
tie (2)
touch (1)
transcribe (2)
transfer (3)
translate (2)
travel (1)
trim (3)
try (4)
turn (1)
type (2)
underline (2)
undress (1)
unload (1)
unpack (1)
unscramble (2)
update (2)
use (2)
vacuum (1)
videotape (2)
visit (1)
volunteer (1)
vomit (1)
vote (2)
wait (1)
walk (1)
wash (1)
watch (1)
water (1)
wave (2)
weed (1)
weigh (1)
wipe (2)
work (1)
wrap (3)
yell (1)

Verb Guide

Irregular Verbs

These verbs have irregular endings in the past and/or the past participle.

The Oxford Picture Dictionary List of Irregular Verbs

simple	past	past participle	simple	past	past participle
be	was	been	make	made	made
beat	beat	beaten	meet	met	met
become	became	become	pay	paid	paid
bend	bent	bent	picnic	picnicked	picnicked
bleed	bled	bled	proofread	proofread	proofread
blow	blew	blown	put	put	put
break	broke	broken	quit	quit	quit
bring	brought	brought	read	read	read
buy	bought	bought	rewind	rewound	rewound
catch	caught	caught	rewrite	rewrote	rewritten
choose	chose	chosen	ride	rode	ridden
come	came	come	run	ran	run
cut	cut	cut	say	said	said
do	did	done	see	saw	seen
draw	drew	drawn	seek	sought	sought
drink	drank	drunk	sell	sold	sold
drive	drove	driven	send	sent	sent
eat	ate	eaten	set	set	set
fall	fell	fallen	sew	sewed	sewn
feed	fed	fed	shake	shook	shaken
feel	felt	felt	shoot	shot	shot
find	found	found	show	showed	shown
fly	flew	flown	sing	sang	sung
freeze	froze	frozen	sit	sat	sat
get	got	gotten	speak	spoke	spoken
give	gave	given	stand	stood	stood
go	went	gone	steal	stole	stolen
hang	hung	hung	sweep	swept	swept
have	had	had	swim	swam	swum
hear	heard	heard	swing	swung	swung
hide	hid	hidden	take	took	taken
hit	hit	hit	teach	taught	taught
hold	held	held	think	thought	thought
keep	kept	kept	throw	threw	thrown
lay	laid	laid	wake	woke	woken
leave	left	left	win	won	won
lend	lent	lent	withdraw	withdrew	withdrawn
let	let	let	write	wrote	written
lose	lost	lost			

Index

Index Key

donut **79**–15
  donut shop **131**–17
door **46**–4 🔑
  door chain **51**–34 🔑
  door lock **163**–25 🔑
  doorbell **53**–14
  doorknob **53**–12
  doorman **192**–1
  front door **53**–11 🔑
  garage door **53**–7 🔑
  revolving door **192**–2
  screen door **53**–15 🔑
  sliding glass door **53**–18 🔑
  storm door **53**–10 🔑
  2-door car **160** ✦
dorm / dormitory **52**–8
dosage **114**–6
double 🔑
  double bed **192**–14 🔑
  double boiler **78**–8
double-click 210–H
down 🔑
  break down 166–F
  down jacket **90**–16
  down vest **90**–14
  downhill skiing **233**–1
  drop-down menu **213**–15
  put down 6–J
  sit down 6–F 🔑
  walk down **157**–D
downstairs **51** ✦🔑
DOWNTOWN **126**–**127** 🔑
drag 210–J 🔑
drain **57**–7
drama **242**–12 🔑 AWL
drapes **56**–16
draw 8–F, **111**–F, **207**–E 🔑
drawer **54**–23, **58**–2, **59**–6 🔑
dress **86**–3, **88**–5, **89**–20 🔑
  dress socks **91**–9 🔑
  dressmaker **100**–1
  dressmaker's dummy **100**–2
dress 36–H, **179**–B
dressed **38**–D
dresser **58**–1
Dressings **80**
dribble 236–J
drill **194**–8, **196**–9
  drill bit **194**–28
drill 120–D
drink **11**–J
  do not drink 114–F 🔑
  don't drink and **drive 146**–G 🔑
  drink fluids **116**–C
drip **123**–25
dripping 63–17
drive **190**–15, **190**–19, **190**–25,
  190–27
  drive-thru window **130**–11
  driveway **53**–8
drive 🔑
  don't **drink** and **drive 146**–G 🔑
  drive a truck **176**–E 🔑

drive through **157**–K 🔑
drive to work **38**–I 🔑
driver **156**–21, **173**–61 🔑
  designated drivers **146** ✦
  driver's license **40**–4, **138**–9 🔑 AWL
  driver's license number **138**–11 🔑
  Phillips screwdriver **194**–31
  screwdriver **194**–30
driving **145**–5 🔑
drop 🔑
  drop cloth **195**–54 🔑
  drop-down menu **213**–15 🔑
  post office lobby drop **137**–11 🔑
drop off 38–G
dropper **207**–45
drops **115**–31 🔑
drought **149**–11
drown 118–I
drugs **118**–K, **145**–6 🔑
drums **244**–16 🔑
drumsticks **70**–23
drunk driving **145**–5 🔑
dry **101**–18 🔑
  dry cleaners **130**–2
  dry erase marker **7**–17
  drywall **196**–19
dry 60–N, **108**–H 🔑
Dry Measures **75** 🔑
dryer **50**–13, **101**–4
  blow dryer **33**–21, **108**–18
  dryer sheets **101**–5
duck **70**–18, **220**–13
duct tape **195**–49 🔑
dummy **100**–2
dump truck **160**–19 🔑
dune **214**–5
duplex **52** ✦
During an Emergency **151** 🔑
dust 🔑
  dust ruffle **58**–17
  dust storm **13**–20 🔑
  dustpan **61**–17
dust 60–A
duster **61**–1
DVD **135**–19 🔑
  DVD and CD-ROM drive **190**–15 🔑
  DVD player **240**–11 🔑
dye 33–D

eagle **220**–10
ear **105**–12 🔑
  ear infection **112**–3 🔑
  earache **110**–3
  earbuds / in-ear headphones **240**–5
  earmuffs **90**–13, **197**–16
  earplugs **197**–15
  pierced ear **32**–17
  pierced earrings **95**–36
early **19**–22 🔑
Earth **215**–3 🔑
earthquake **148**–5
easel **239**–18
east **159**–4 🔑

Eastern time **19**–32
easy **23**–23, **76**–11 🔑
  easy chair **56**–22 🔑
Easy Chicken Soup **77** 🔑
eat 11–I 🔑
  eat a healthy diet **116**–F 🔑
  eat breakfast **38**–E 🔑
  eat dinner **39**–S 🔑
  eat out **82** ✦🔑
eater
  weed eater **186**–12
e-book **135**–18
eclipse **215**–16
edit 203–I AWL
education 🔑
  basic education **175**–1 🔑
  continuing education **175**–7 🔑
  physical education **201**–17 🔑 AWL
eel **218**–12
eggplants **69**–23
eggs **66**–7 🔑
  eggbeater **78**–20
  eggs over easy **76**–11 🔑
  eggs sunny-side up **76**–10 🔑
  hard-boiled eggs **76**–8 🔑
  poached eggs **76**–9
  scrambled eggs **76**–7
Eggs **76** 🔑
eight **16**
eighteen **16**
eighteenth **16**
eighth **16**
eightieth **16**
eighty **16**
elastic bandage **119**–13 🔑
elbow **106**–12 🔑
elderly **32**–3 🔑
elected **143**–M 🔑
  elected official **143**–12 🔑
Election **143** 🔑
  election results **143**–11 🔑
elective **201** ✦
electric **118**–F 🔑
  electric can opener **54**–14
  electric drill **194**–8
  electric keyboard **244**–18 🔑
  electric mixer **54**–25
  electric pencil sharpener **189**–26
  electric shaver **109**–26
  electric vehicle / EV **160**–2 🔑
electrical 🔑
  electrical hazard **198**–6
  electrical tape **195**–43 🔑
electrician **62**–9
electron **207**–30
electronics
  electronics repairperson **171**–24
  electronics store **133**–20
ELECTRONICS AND PHOTOGRAPHY
  240–**241** 🔑
elementary school **200**–2 🔑
elephant **223**–42
elevator **50**–9, **133**–21, **192**–9 🔑

261

hard **23**–5, **23**–24 🔑
  external hard drive **190**–27 🔑
  hard drive **190**–19 🔑
  hard hat **92**–1, **197**–9 🔑
  hard-boiled eggs **76**–8 🔑
hardware store **152**–4
harmonica **244**–21
harvest 187–B
hash browns **80**–3
hatchback **160**–6
hats **90**–1, **95**–11 🔑
  chef's hat **93**–28
  cowboy hat **92**–18
  hard hat **92**–1, **197**–9 🔑
  ski hat **90**–11
  straw hat **90**–23
have 🔑
  have a baby **41**–L 🔑
  have a conversation **11**–L 🔑
  have a flat tire **166**–C 🔑
  have a heart attack **118**–D 🔑
  have a picnic **230**–D
  have an allergic reaction **118**–E 🔑 AWL
  have dinner **39**–S 🔑
  have regular checkups **116**–H
Hawaii-Aleutian time **19**–27
hay **187**–18
hazard **198**–6
  hazard lights **163**–36
Hazardous Materials **197**
hazardous waste **224**–12
Hazards **197**
head **104**–1 🔑
  Bluetooth headset **14**–14
  head chef **193**–7
  head of lettuce **69**–32
  headache **110**–1 🔑
  headband **90**–3
  headboard **58**–10
  headlight **162**–7
  headline **135**–7
  headphones **6**–8, **240**–4, **240**–5, **240**–6
  headset **14**–13, **191**–35
  headwaiter **193**–12
  headwrap **90**–7
  letterhead **189**–42
  overhead compartment **165**–13
headquarters / corporate offices **184**–1 🔑 AWL
health 🔑
  health history form **111**–4 🔑
  health insurance card **111**–3 🔑
HEALTH **116**–**117** 🔑
HEALTH FAIR **124**–**125** 🔑
HEALTH INSURANCE **121** 🔑
Health Problems **117** 🔑
hear 106–B 🔑
hearing 🔑
  hearing aid **117**–10 🔑 AWL
  hearing impaired **32**–12
  hearing loss **117**–2 🔑
heart **107**–38, **245**–6 🔑
  have a heart attack **118**–D 🔑
  heart disease **113**–28 🔑

hearts **239**–31 🔑
heat wave **13**–15 🔑
heating pad **115**–13
heavy **23**–13, **32**–7, **97**–27 🔑
hedge clippers **186**–11
heel **94**–22, **106**–24 🔑
  high heels **89**–21, **95**–25, **97**–32 🔑
  low heels **97**–31 🔑
height **17**–16, **32**–5 🔑
Height **32** 🔑
Heimlich maneuver **119**–19
helicopter **155**–9
helmet **93**–23, **237**–19
help 8–J, **151**–G 🔑
Help with Health Problems **117** 🔑
hem **100**–8
hen **221**–8
hepatitis **112**–9
herbal tea **81**–40 🔑
herbs **84**–9
hibiscus **217**–12
hide 246–D 🔑
high **97**–32 🔑
  high blood pressure **113**–24 🔑
  high chair **37**–6, **82**–3 🔑
  high heels **89**–21, **95**–25 🔑
  high school **200**–4 🔑
  high-rise **129**–13
  high visibility safety vest **92**–4 🔑 AWL
  junior high school **200**–3 🔑
  knee highs **91**–12 🔑
highlighter **7**–25
highway **159**–9 🔑
  highway marker **158**–17
hiking **232**–7
  hiking boots **95**–31 🔑
hills **214**–16 🔑
  downhill skiing **233**–1
hip **107**–27 🔑
hip-hop **243**–26
hippopotamus **223**–43
hire 144–B 🔑
hired hand **187**–20 🔑
Historical Terms **209** 🔑
history **111**–4, **201**–12 🔑
HISTORY **209** 🔑
hit 236–B 🔑
HIV / AIDS **113**–21
HOBBIES AND GAMES **238**–**239** 🔑
hockey **235**–14
  hockey stick **237**–11
hold 36–A 🔑
holder
  candle holder **56**–21
  policyholder **121**–5
  potholders **78**–29
  toothbrush holder **57**–24
holiday **22**–7, **22**–8 🔑
HOLIDAYS **245** 🔑
Holidays **22** 🔑
holly **216**–19
home **52**–7, **52**–12 🔑
  home healthcare aide **171**–32

home improvement store **129**–20 🔑
home phone **4**–12 🔑
homemaker **172**–33
homesick **43**–20
HOME **46**–**49** 🔑
honest **178**–4 🔑
honeybee **220**–26
hood **162**–4
Hood **162**
hoodie **89**–22
hoof / hooves **222**–17
hook **194**–39 🔑
  eye hook **194**–40 🔑
  hook and eye **99**–27 🔑
  hook and loop fastener **99**–29
horn **163**–32, **222**–21, **244**–11 🔑
  French horn **244**–13
horror story **243**–17 🔑
horse **221**–4 🔑
  horse racing **234**–19 🔑
  horseback riding **232**–9 🔑
  seahorse **218**–13
hose **53**–21
  pantyhose **91**–18
hospital **127**–9, **158**–18 🔑
  hospital bed **123**–22 🔑
  hospital gown **123**–19
HOSPITAL **122**–**123** 🔑
Hospital Room **123** 🔑
Hospital Staff **122** 🔑
hostess **82**–2
hot **13**–3, **42**–1 🔑
  hot cereal **80**–9
  hot dog **79**–6
  hot water **57**–9 🔑
  hot water bottle **115**–15 🔑
hotel **126**–3 🔑
A HOTEL **192** 🔑
hour **18**–1 🔑
house 🔑
  courthouse **127**–13
  dollhouse **59**–18
  House of Representatives **140**–3
  house painter **172**–46 🔑
  house salad **80**–15 🔑
  housekeeper **172**–34, **192**–20
  housekeeping cart **192**–19
  houseplant **56**–4, **217**–27
  townhouse **52**–6
  two-story house **52** ✦🔑
  warehouse **184**–3, **185**–7
  White House **140**–7
House **49** 🔑
HOUSE AND YARD **53** 🔑
HOUSEHOLD PROBLEMS AND REPAIRS
  62–**63** 🔑
HOUSEWORK **60**
housing **52**–11 🔑
hub **190**–26
hubcap **162**–9
hug 2–F
human resources **184**–4 🔑 AWL
humid **13**–17

273

toilet **57**–21 🔑
    toilet brush **57**–20 🔑
    toilet paper **57**–19, **150**–13 🔑
token **156**–10
tomatoes **69**–6 🔑
tomorrow **20**–6 🔑
tongs **78**–23, **207**–44
tongue **106**–8 🔑
too
    too big **97**–38 🔑
    too expensive **97**–44 🔑
    too small **97**–37 🔑
tool belt **92**–3 🔑
TOOLS AND BUILDING SUPPLIES **194**–**195** 🔑
tooth / teeth **106**–7 🔑
    pull a tooth **120**–F 🔑
    toothache **110**–2
    toothbrush **57**–23, **109**–22
    toothbrush holder **57**–24
    toothpaste **109**–23
top **88**–7, **89**–24 🔑
torn **97**–41 🔑
tornado **149**–15
torso **106** ✦
tortoise **219**–41
total **27**–9 🔑
tote bag **94**–19
touch 106–E 🔑
touch screen / audio display **163**–37 🔑
tow truck **160**–14
towel 🔑
    bath towel **57**–16 🔑
    dish towel **61**–22 🔑
    hand towel **57**–17 🔑
    paper towels **54**–3 🔑
    towel rack **57**–15
towelettes **150**–12
tower **190**–7 🔑
town **52**–3 🔑
    town car **156**–20 🔑
    townhouse **52**–6
toy 🔑
    toy chest **59**–16 🔑
    toy store **132**–5 🔑
Toys and Games **59** 🔑
track **5**–21, **156**–14 🔑
    track and field **234**–18 🔑
track pad **190**–24
tractor **187**–9
    tractor-trailer **160**–15
traffic light **130**–8 🔑
TRAFFIC SIGNS **158** 🔑
tragedy **243**–14
trailer **160**–15, **160**–17
train **154**–7, **239**–27 🔑
Train Station **156** 🔑
training **175**–3, **175**–9, **175**–12 🔑
    training pants **37**–16 🔑
Training **175** 🔑
transcribe 177–C
transfer **156**–5 AWL
transfer 177–O 🔑 AWL
translate 8–C 🔑

translator **172**–35
Transmission **163** AWL
TRANSPORTATION **154**–**156** 🔑 AWL
Transportation **156** 🔑 AWL
trash 🔑
    trash bags **61**–24 🔑
    trash bin **51**–23
    trash chute **51**–26
travel 41–P 🔑
travel agency **133**–14 🔑
tray **55**–17, **83**–10
    tray table **165**–21
Tree **216** 🔑
trees **245**–16 🔑
TREES AND PLANTS **216** 🔑
trench coat **90**–21
trial **142**–5 🔑
triangle **205**–32 🔑
tricycle **230**–12
trigonometry **204**–18
trim 186–B
Trim **99**
trip **156**–16, **156**–17 🔑
tripe **70**–8
tripod **241**–20
trombone **244**–10
trout **71**–1
trowel **186**–10, **196**–13
truck **154**–6 🔑
    dump truck **160**–19
    fire truck **148**–10 🔑
    garbage truck **129**–22 🔑
    hand truck **185**–11 🔑
    pickup truck **160**–12
    tank truck **160**–20 🔑
    tow truck **160**–14
    truck driver **173**–61 🔑
TRUCKS **160** 🔑
trumpet **244**–11
trunk **162**–11, **216**–4, **223**–47
Trunk **162**
trunks
    swimming trunks **90**–22
try on 95–C 🔑
TSA agent **164**–5 🔑
T-shirt **86**–4
tsunami **149**–17
tub
    bathtub **57**–2
tuba **244**–12
tube **74**–24, **207**–42
tuberculosis (TB) **113**–23
tubes **74**–12
Tuesday **20**–10 🔑
tulip **217**–11
tuna **71**–7, **72**–19, **218**–8
tuner **240**–13
turbulence **165**–22
turkey **70**–17, **245**–14
    roasted turkey **76**–4
    smoked turkey **71**–25
turn **158**–5, **158**–7, **158**–8 🔑
    turn signal **162**–6, **163**–34 🔑

turnstile **156**–8
turntable **240**–12
turn 🔑
    turn in 203–M 🔑
    turn left **159**–C 🔑
    turn off 11–P, **179**–G, **225**–G 🔑
    turn on 11–D, **147**–A 🔑
    turn right **159**–B 🔑
turnips **69**–16
turquoise **24**–9
turtle **219**–42
    turtleneck **96**–9
tusk **223**–48
tuxedo **89**–17
TV / television **56**–6 🔑
    big-screen TV **50**–14 🔑
    flat-panel TV **240**–8 🔑
    flat-screen TV **240**–8 🔑
TV Programs **242**
tweezers **119**–5
twelfth **16**
twelve **16**
twentieth **16**
twenty **16**
    twenty after one **18**–10 🔑
    twenty dollars **26**–10
    twenty to two **18**–12
    twenty-first **16**
    twenty-five **16**
    25 percent **17**–11 🔑
    twenty-four **16**
    twenty-one **16**
    twenty-three **16**
    twenty-two **16**
twice a week **20**–23 🔑
twig **216**–1
twins **28**–1 🔑
two **16**
    2 x 4 (two by four) **195**–19
    two-story house **52** ✦🔑
    two-way radio **197**–22 🔑
type 4–D, **176**–R, **210**–C
    type a letter **177**–A 🔑
    type in a phrase **212**–B 🔑
    type in a question **212**–C 🔑
    type the password again **211**–Q 🔑
    type the subject **211**–V
    type the verification code **211**–R 🔑
Types of Charges **15** 🔑
Types of Health Problems **117** 🔑
Types of Material **98**–**99** 🔑
Types of Math **204** 🔑
Types of Medication **115**
Types of Movies **243** 🔑
Types of Music **243** 🔑
Types of Training **175** 🔑
Types of TV Programs **242**

ugly **23**–22 🔑
umbrella **90**–17, **231**–14 🔑
umpire **235** ✦
uncle **34**–8 🔑
uncomfortable **42**–9 🔑

Research Bibliography

The authors and publisher wish to acknowledge the contribution of the following educators for their research on vocabulary development, which has helped inform the principles underlying *OPD*.

Burt, M., J. K. Peyton, and R. Adams. *Reading and Adult English Language Learners: A Review of the Research.* Washington, DC: Center for Applied Linguistics, 2003.

Coady, J. "Research on ESL/EFL Vocabulary Acquisition: Putting it in Context." In *Second Language Reading and Vocabulary Learning,* edited by T. Huckin, M. Haynes, and J. Coady. Norwood, NJ: Ablex, 1993.

de la Fuente, M. J. "Negotiation and Oral Acquisition of L2 Vocabulary: The Roles of Input and Output in the Receptive and Productive Acquisition of Words." *Studies in Second Language Acquisition* 24 (2002): 81–112.

DeCarrico, J. "Vocabulary learning and teaching." In *Teaching English as a Second or Foreign Language,* edited by M. Celcia-Murcia. 3rd ed. Boston: Heinle & Heinle, 2001.

Ellis, R. *The Study of Second Language Acquisition.* Oxford: Oxford University Press, 1994.

Folse, K. *Vocabulary Myths: Applying Second Language Research to Classroom Teaching.* Ann Arbor, MI: University of Michigan Press, 2004.

Gairns, R. and S. Redman. *Working with Words: A Guide to Teaching and Learning Vocabulary.* Cambridge: Cambridge University Press, 1986.

Gass, S. M. and M. J. A. Torres. "Attention When?: An Investigation of the Ordering Effect of Input and Interaction." *Studies in Second Language Acquisition* 27 (Mar 2005): 1–31.

Henriksen, Birgit. "Three Dimensions of Vocabulary Development." *Studies in Second Language Acquisition* 21 (1999): 303–317.

Koprowski, Mark. "Investigating the Usefulness of Lexical Phrases in Contemporary Coursebooks." *Oxford ELT Journal* 59(4) (2005): 322–332.

McCrostie, James. "Examining Learner Vocabulary Notebooks." *Oxford ELT Journal* 61 (July 2007): 246–255.

Nation, P. *Learning Vocabulary in Another Language.* Cambridge: Cambridge University Press, 2001.

National Center for ESL Literacy Education Staff. *Adult English Language Instruction in the 21st Century.* Washington, DC: Center for Applied Linguistics, 2003.

National Reading Panel. *Teaching Children to Read: An Evidenced-Based Assessment of the Scientific Research Literature on Reading and its Implications on Reading Instruction.* 2000. https://www.nichd.nih.gov/publications/pubs/nrp/documents/report.pdf.

Newton, J. "Options for Vocabulary Learning through Communication Tasks." *Oxford ELT Journal* 55(1) (2001): 30–37.

Prince, P. "Second Language Vocabulary Learning: The Role of Context Versus Translations as a Function of Proficiency." *Modern Language Journal* 80(4) (1996): 478–493.

Savage, K. L., ed. *Teacher Training Through Video - ESL Techniques: Early Production.* White Plains, NY: Longman Publishing Group, 1992.

Schmitt, N. *Vocabulary in Language Teaching.* Cambridge: Cambridge University Press, 2000.

Smith, C. B. *Vocabulary Instruction and Reading Comprehension.* Bloomington, IN: ERIC Clearinghouse on Reading English and Communication, 1997.

Wood, K. and J. Josefina Tinajero. "Using Pictures to Teach Content to Second Language Learners." *Middle School Journal* 33 (2002): 47–51.